COLUMBIA UNIVERSITY BIOLOGICAL SERIES. I.

FROM THE GREEKS TO DARWIN

AN OUTLINE OF THE DEVELOPMENT OF THE EVOLUTION IDEA

BY

HENRY FAIRFIELD OSBORN, Sc.D.

DA COSTA PROFESSOR OF ZOÖLOGY IN COLUMBIA UNIVERSITY; CURATOR IN THE AMERICAN MUSEUM OF NATURAL HISTORY

SECOND EDITION

New York
THE MACMILLAN COMPANY
LONDON: MACMILLAN & CO., LTD.
1905

All rights reserved

This important reprint was made from an old and scarce book.

Therefore, it may have defects such as missing pages, erroneous pagination, blurred pages, missing text, poor pictures, markings, marginalia and other issues beyond our control.

Because this is such an important and rare work, we believe it is best to reproduce this book regardless of its original condition.

Thank you for your understanding and enjoy this unique book!

TO

MY REVERED TEACHER IN PHILOSOPHY

James McCosh

EX-PRESIDENT OF PRINCETON COLLEGE

PREFACE.

THIS volume has grown out of lectures first delivered in Princeton in 1890, upon the period between Buffon and Darwin, and completed in a fuller course delivered in Columbia in 1893, which covered also the period before Buffon. When I began the study, my object was to bring forward the many strong and true features of pre-Darwinian Evolution, which are so generally passed over or misunderstood. When all the materials were brought together from the earliest times, the evidence of continuity in the development of the idea became more clear, and to trace these lines of development has gradually become the central motive of these lectures. More thorough research, which may, perhaps, be stimulated by these outlines will, I believe, strengthen this evidence.

I am greatly indebted to my friends Professor George Macloskie and Professor Alexander T. Ormond for assistance and critical advice in connection with the revision of the proofs.

H. F. O.

COLUMBIA COLLEGE, July 11th, 1894.

CONTENTS.

		PAGE
I.	THE ANTICIPATION AND INTERPRETATION OF NATURE.	1
	Preliminary Survey. Environment of the Evolution idea. Periods of its development. Nature of the idea. The scientific method of thought. The Advance of Philosophy. Advance of Zoölogy and Botany. Embryology.	
II.	AMONG THE GREEKS	29
	Conditions of Greek thought. The Greek Periods. Ionians and Eleatics: Thales, Anaximander, Anaximenes, Xenophanes. The Physicists: Heraclitus, Empedocles, Democritus, Anaxagoras. Aristotle and his followers. Pliny, Epicurus, Lucretius. The legacy of the Greeks to later Evolution.	
III.	THE THEOLOGIANS AND NATURAL PHILOSOPHERS	69
	Transition from Greek Philosophy to Christian Theology. The Fathers and Schoolmen: Gregory, Augustine, Erigena, Aquinas. Arabic Science and Philosophy: Avicenna, Avempace, Abubacer. Bruno and Suarez. The awakening of Science. Characteristics of Evolution in Philosophy. The Natural Philosophers: Bacon, Descartes, Leibnitz, Kant, Lessing, Herder, Schelling.	
IV.	THE EVOLUTIONISTS OF THE EIGHTEENTH CENTURY	106
	The two series of Evolutionists. The speculative Evolutionists: Duret, Kircher, Maupertuis, Diderôt, Bonnet, De Maillet, Robinet, Oken. The Naturalists: Linnæus, Buffon, E. Darwin.	
V.	FROM LAMARCK TO ST. HILAIRE	152
	Erasmus Darwin and Lamarck. Lamarck. Goethe. Treviranus. Cuvier. Geoffroy St. Hilaire. Discussion between Cuvier and St. Hilaire. Bory de St. Vincent. Isidore St. Hilaire. Decline of the Evolution idea.	
VI.	DARWIN	209
	The first half-century. Miscellaneous writers. The Embryologists: Meckel, Baer, Serres. The followers of Buffon: Herbert, Buch, Haldeman, Spencer. The Progressionists: Chambers, Owen. The Selectionists: Wells, Matthew, St. Hilaire, Naudin, Wallace. Darwin. Darwin and Wallace in 1858. Retrospect.	

Wir können bei Betrachtung des Weltgebäudes in seiner weitesten Ausdehnung, in seiner letzten Teilbarkeit uns der Vorstellung nicht erwehren, dass dem Ganzen eine *Idee* zum Grunde liege, wornach Gott in der Natur, die Natur in Gott von Ewigkeit zu Ewigkeit schaffen und wirken möge. Anschauung, Betrachtung, Nachdenken führen uns näher an jene Geheimnisse. Wir erdreisten uns und wagen auch Ideen, wir bescheiden uns und bilden Begriffe, die analog jenen Urdingen sein möchten. GOETHE.

I.

THE ANTICIPATION AND INTERPRETATION OF NATURE.

There are and can exist but two ways of investigating and discovering truth. The one hurries on rapidly from the senses and particulars to the most general axioms, and from them, as principles and their supposed indisputable truth, derives and discovers the intermediate axioms. This is the way now in use. The other constructs its axioms from the senses and particulars by ascending continually and gradually till it finally arrives at the most general axioms, which is the true but unattempted way.

We are wont to call that human reasoning which we apply to Nature the *anticipation of Nature* (as being rash and premature), and that which is properly deduced from things the *interpretation of Nature*. — BACON, *Novum Organum*.

In the growth of the numerous lesser ideas which have converged into the central idea of the history of life by Evolution, we find ancient pedigrees for all that we are apt to consider modern. Evolution has reached its present fulness by slow additions in twenty-four centuries. When the truths and absurdities of Greek, mediæval, and sixteenth to nineteenth century speculation and observation are brought together, it becomes clear that they form a continuous whole, that the influences of early upon later thought are greater than has been believed, that Darwin owes more even to the Greeks than we have ever recognized. It is true that until 1858 speculation far outran fact, and that the development of the idea was at times arrested and even retrogressive; yet the conviction grows with inquiry that the Evolution law was reached not by any decided leap, but <u>by the progressive development</u> of every subordinate idea connected with it, until it was recognized as a whole by Lamarck, and later by Darwin.

In order to prove this, I endeavour to trace back some of these lesser ideas to their sources, and to bring the comparatively little known early evolutionists into their true relief as original thinkers and contributors, or mere borrowers and imitators. This is possible only because such search has already been very ably made among certain authors and in certain periods by other writers, to whom I am largely indebted for whatever success I have attained in this first attempt to cover the whole period and to establish the evidence of continuity.

Little national bias has been shown in the search for anticipations of Darwin among his precursors; as one instance, the highest praises of Lamarck have been sounded in Germany, and of Goethe in France. The greatest defects I find in the historical literature of this subject are the lack of sense of proportion as to the original merits of different writers, and the non-appreciation of the continuity of evolution thought. In general, we need more critical and thorough work than has yet been given us. Many heralded anticipations are not anticipations at all, if we speak of Darwinism in the restricted sense and not as all-embracing. Others are genuine, yet they consist of speculative ideas which had been retold or rediscovered several times over, as in the case of the law of Survival of the Fittest.

The estimates I have reached as to several of the founders of the idea are therefore different from those advanced by others. By considering together all the historic stages of the development even in a brief manner, we can trace the continuity, the increasing momentum of the idea, and consequently the increasing indebtedness to previous suggestion. We can see how many of the prophecies were themselves foretold. Most obvious is the fact that Greek speculations and suggestions were borrowed and used over and over again as if original, continuity in the lesser ideas which cluster around Evolution being quite as marked as in the main idea. To fully follow out all such genetic threads would, however, require a far more exhaustive research than this aims to be.

Apart from suggestion we meet with many remarkable coincidences in the lines of independent and even simultaneous discovery, notably those between Erasmus Darwin and Lamarck, between Lamarck and Treviranus, before we reach the crowning and most exceptional case of Darwin and Wallace. At different periods similar facts were leading men to similar conclusions, and we gather many fine illustrations of the force of unconscious induction. Means of intercommunication were slow, and we should advance cautiously before concluding that any of the greater evolutionists were dealing with borrowed ideas.

Finally, I have attempted to estimate each author from his thought as a whole, before placing him in the scales with his predecessors, contemporaries, and successors. When we study single passages, we are often led widely afield. Haeckel, for example, appears to have far overstated the relative merits of Oken, a writer who shines forth brightly in certain passages, and goes under a cloud in others, his sum total being obscure and weak. Krause has placed Erasmus Darwin over Lamarck without sufficient consideration. Huxley has treated Treviranus and Lamarck with almost equal respect; they are really found to be most unequal when tested by their approach to the modern conception of Evolution. We must inquire into the sources or grounds of the conclusions advanced by each writer, how far derived from others, how far from observation of Nature, and consider the soundness of each as well as his suggestiveness and originality, before we can judge fairly what permanent links he may have added or welded into the chain of thought.

Outlines of the Whole Development.

The history, as a whole, before Darwin, at first sight appears to have been mainly the anticipation of Nature; but closer examination reveals much genuine interpretation of Nature. Before the middle of this century, in fact, natural science was not ready for Evolution on the inductive line. The way had to be paved for it; one proof of this is found in the failure of the strong Evolution movement in France during the latter part of the last, and beginning of this century. In the middle of this century came the time and the man who ranks as the great central thinker. Under the impetus of Darwin, the first steps were to establish, as a natural law, what had ranked as an hypothesis or theory, and this has been most thoroughly done in the last thirty-five years. We are now taking our uncertain steps in search of the separate factors of this law, and cannot foresee when these will be completed. 'Before and after Darwin' will always be the *ante et post urbem conditam* of biological history. Before Darwin, the theory; after Darwin, the factors.

We remember that there are usually three stages in connection with the discovery of a law of Nature; first, that of dim suggestion in pure speculation, with eyes closed to facts; second, that of clear statement as a tentative or working hypothesis in an explanation of certain facts; and finally, the proof or demonstration. Darwin came in for the proof, profiting richly by the hard struggles of his predecessors over the first two stages. Lamarck has lately risen in popular knowledge as having propounded Evolution, but among his contemporaries and predecessors in France, Germany, and England, we find Buffon, Erasmus Darwin, Goethe, Treviranus, and searching for their inspiration, we are led back to the natural philosophers, beginning with Bacon, and ending with Herder. Among these men we find the second birth or renaissance of the idea, and among the Greeks its first birth.

Evolution, as a natural explanation of the origin of the higher forms of life, succeeded the old mythology and autochthony in Greece, and developed from the teachings of Thales and Anaximander into those of Aristotle. This great philosopher had a general conception of the origin of higher species by descent from lower, yet he could not know of any actual Evolution series, such as we have derived from Paleontology. He also considered certain of the factors of Evolution underlying the general law, and it is startling to find him, over two thousand years ago, clearly stating, and then rejecting, the theory of the Survival of the Fittest as an explanation of the evolution of adaptive structures.

The Greek natural history literature, from beginning to end, is a continuous source of pleasure and surprise. Amid wide differences of opinion as to how far the Greeks actually anticipated later discoveries, the true conclusion is, that they anticipated many of our modern theories by suggestion; thus they carried the Evolution idea well into its suggestive stage, which was so much ground gained for those who took it up in Europe. Greek speculations greatly hastened the final result, although, judged by modern scientific standards, they arose mainly as a series of happy conjectures. We know that Greek philosophy tinctured early Christian theology; it is not so generally realized that the Aristotelian notion of the development of life led to the true interpretation of the Mosaic account of the Creation.

There was, in fact, a long Greek period in the history of the Evolution idea, extending among the Fathers of the Church, and later, among some of the Schoolmen, in their commentaries upon Creation which accord very closely with the modern theistic conceptions of Evolution. If the orthodoxy of Augustine had remained the teaching of the Church, the final establishment of Evolution would have come far earlier than it did; certainly during the eighteenth instead of the nineteenth century, and the bitter controversy over this truth of Nature would never have arisen. As late as the seventeenth century, the Jesuit Suarez and others contended that the Book of Genesis contained a literal account of the mode of Creation, and thereby Special Creation acquired a firm status as a theory in the contemporary philosophy. Singularly enough, Milton's epics appeared shortly afterwards, exerting an equally profound influence upon English Protestant thought, so that Huxley has aptly termed Special Creation, 'the Miltonic hypothesis.' Thus the opportunity of a free, unchecked development out of natural science was lost.

During the long Middle Ages, the Evolution idea made no advance. Finally it began to retrogress, when Greek natural philosophy shared in the general suppression of the rationalistic movement of thought of Arabic origin. Later the hard and fast conceptions and definitions of species, developed in the rapid rise of systematic Botany and Zoölogy, were grafted upon the Mosaic account of the Creation, establishing a Special Creation theory for the origin of each species. Later still, when it was discovered in Paleontology that species of different kinds had succeeded each other in time, the 'Special' theory was again remodelled to cover a succession of creations extending down almost to the present day. Thus an ecclesiastical dogma developed into a pseudo-scientific theory full of inconsistencies but stoutly maintained by leading zoölogists and botanists.

The history of the central Evolution idea before Darwin therefore follows its rise and fall as the broad explanation of the history of life, which we must throw into contrast with the steady rise of the special knowledge of the lesser ideas which centre in it. As a whole, it rose among the Greeks, declined with the decay of Greek science, was kept alive by Greek influence in Theology, and fell in the opposition to rationalism. When it was first revived in France and Germany, it was either inspired by Greek freedom of speculation and suggestiveness, or permeated by Greek fallacies.

In the first revival the natural philosophers took the lead, followed, in the second, by a series of rashly speculative writers. Then the working and observing naturalists took it up. Considering the Greek movement as the first, this was the second genuine progressive movement towards the Evolution theory; it reached its height with Lamarck, and then declined, or rather failed to make a permanent or widespread impression. In the middle of this century, all the ground gained was apparently but not really lost; science, church, and laity were almost at one upon the Special Creation theory. The open dissenters were comparatively few and very guarded in the expression of their opinions. Young Darwin was among the few who kept before his mind both theories; he met and successfully overcame the great tide of adverse opinion; a conquest which Germany has recognized by rechristening Evolution — *Darwinismus*. Since 1858 more works upon Evolution have appeared each year than in all the centuries previous.

In this more recent history, which I hope to take up in the same spirit in another course, we again trace the rise and fall of certain ideas; even our present thought leaders having their remote parallels in the past. For even amidst our present wealth of facts the impassable boundaries of human thought seem to confine us to unconscious revivals of Greek conceptions. There are many observers, but few who can strike out into the absolutely virgin soil of novel suggestion.

The special phases of Evolution development may accordingly be marked off in the following manner: —

THE ANTICIPATION OF NATURE: GREEK EVOLUTION.

I. 640 B.C.–1600 A.D.

Greek Evolution in Christian Theology; in Arabic Philosophy.

The rise, decline, revival, and final decline of the Greek Natural History and Greek conception of Evolution. Of this period were Thales, Anaximander, Anaximenes, Xenophanes, Heraclitus, Empedocles, Democritus, Anaxagoras, Aristotle, Epicurus, Lucretius, Gregory, Augustine, Bruno, Avempace, Abubacer.

THE INTERPRETATION OF NATURE: MODERN EVOLUTION.

II. 1600–1800 A.D.

Philosophical Evolution.

Emancipation of Botany and Zoölogy from Greek traditions.

The beginnings of *Modern Evolution* as part of a natural order of the universe. Suggestions of inductive Evolution, as based upon the transformation and filiation of species, by the natural philosophers, Bacon, Descartes, Leibnitz, Hume, Kant, Lessing, Herder, Schelling.

Revival of *Greek Evolution* ideas in speculative form by such speculative philosophical writers and naturalists as Maupertuis, Didcrôt, De Maillet, Robinet, Bonnet, Oken.

III. 1730-1850 A.D.

Modern Inductive Evolution, 3d Period: Buffon to St. Hilaire.

Rapid extension of Zoölogy, Botany and Paleontology. Rise and decline of inductive Evolution. Scattered observation and speculation upon the filiation and transformation of species.

Linnæus, Buffon, E. Darwin, Lamarck, Goethe, Treviranus, Geof. St. Hilaire, St. Vincent, Is. St. Hilaire. Miscellaneous writers: Grant, Rafinesque, Virey, Dujardin, d'Halloy, Chevreul, Godron, Leidy, Unger, Carus, Lecoq, Schaafhausen, Wolff, Meckel, Von Baer, Serres, Herbert, Buch, Wells, Matthew, Naudin, Haldeman, Spencer, Chambers, Owen.

IV. 1858-1893 A.D.

Modern Inductive Evolution, 4th Period: Darwin, Wallace.

Evolution established inductively and deductively as a law of Nature. The factor of Natural Selection established. Observation and speculation upon other factors of Evolution.

No sharp lines actually separated these periods; each passed gradually into the next. The decline of Greek, and especially of Aristotelian influence in natural science, was extremely gradual, and was overlapped by the awakening of the spirit of original research upon animals and plants, and of the science of medicine. Similarly, what we may call the Philosophers' period ran insensibly into the Buffon or third period, for the later naturalists began their work contemporaneously with the later philosophers. Perhaps the sharpest transition was at the close of the third period, in which a distinct anti-Evolution school had sprung up and succeeded in firmly entrenching itself, so that Darwin and Wallace began the present era with some abruptness.

ENVIRONMENT OF THE EVOLUTION IDEA.

As we have seen in this *résumé*, the idea had a long struggle for growth and existence in the twenty-four centuries between Thales and Darwin, yet it never wholly suspended animation. I may emphasize again the standpoint of these lectures, that the final conception of Evolution is to be regarded as a cluster of many subsidiary ideas, which slowly evolved in the environment of advancing human knowledge. Like an animal or plant, made up of many different parts which have been added one by one along the ages, we can take up this history as we should a bit of biological research; consider the idea as living and still growing, and seek the first stages of each of its parts. These we will find in the earliest guesses as to the origin of life from matter; in conjectures about development and reproduction; in early observed evidences of heredity, degeneration, variation, and of the affiliation between organisms; in the first appreciation of environment and its influences, of internal changes in the body and their influences, of adaptation or fitness, of the survival of the fittest organisms, and finally of the survival of the fittest organs. As each part of every organism has begun as a rudiment and followed its own independent history, so each of these subsidiary ideas rose in a crude form, and became increasingly clear and definite.

We have then three objects in view: first, to follow the broad idea of Evolution as a natural law; second, to trace back the birth and development of each of its parts; third, to keep constantly in mind the changing environment of knowledge and prejudice. The uncongenial influences were by no means confined to those mentioned above; the introduction and long persistence of scientific fallacies, such as Abiogenesis, the uncertain methods of scientific thinking, the limited knowledge of Nature, and especially of animal and plant life, are all to be considered. As these were cleared away, the environment became more congenial, and the idea began its unchecked development.

If we look at the idea in itself, we first distinguish between the law of Evolution as an explanation of the origin of all forms of life; second, the evidences for such a law, and third, the theories and conjectures as to the natural causes or factors underlying this law or constituting it. The full conception came very late. Apparently Lamarck was the first to grasp Evolution in its modern significance, and to see the analogy between the past history of life and a great widely branching tree, having its roots in the simplest organisms, its shorter branches in the lower, and its longer branches in the higher forms of life. According to this now familiar analogy, the living forms of to-day are the terminal twigs of great branches which represent the lines of extinct ancestors. These branches united near the trunk with others, whilst still other branches, with their terminal branchlets, have entirely died out in past time. Or, to trace the history upwards instead of downwards and begin at the roots, the lower branches of the tree are comparatively few, and represent the great classes of animals which divided and subdivided into orders, sub-orders, families, genera, species, and so on.

Prior to Lamarck this branching nature of descent was only very crudely perceived. This was because Aristotle's general view that the existing forms of life constituted a scale of ascent from the polyps to man, had been revived in different aspects, such as the 'perfection chain' of Leibnitz, or the famous '*échelle*' of Bonnet. It is evident that the modern conception grew out of the discovery of the extinction of earlier and intermediate forms of life such as came from Paleontology, and that it is essentially different from the ancient 'ladder' or 'chain' conception, which regarded the existing terminal twigs of the tree as directly affiliated to each other, rather than through the extinct earlier branches. Pre-Lamarckian Evolution was mainly a conception of the gradual rise of higher forms of life by descent and modification from lower forms still existing. This, in contrast with the notions of sudden production of life from the earth or by Special Creation, was based upon slow development, and had the distinction always of being a naturalistic explanation.

The variety of terms under which Evolution has figured, to a certain extent mark the chapters in its history. In France, the early terms '*transmutation*' and '*filiation*' have partly given way to the more modern '*transformisme*.' In England, Evolution has been known as the 'doctrine of derivation,' as the 'development hypothesis,' and as the 'descent theory.' For the first half of this century, Evolution was known mainly as the Lamarckian theory, just as later it universally became the Darwinian theory; while very recently 'Lamarckism' and 'Darwinism' have each acquired special meanings, and the comprehensive term 'Evolution,' first used by St. Hilaire in this sense, has come in as the permanent designation of the law. This embraces more and more as our knowledge advances, so we speak even of the first naturalistic views of the gradual succession of species as Evolution because they contained the idea in the germ.

The Scientific Method of Thought.

The slow discovery of scientific modes of observation and thought constituted a very important feature in the environment of the Evolution idea. Now working, as a matter of course, by the inductive-deductive or observe-and-guess method, first observing a few facts, for a preliminary induction or 'working hypothesis' to apply tentatively to certain classes of facts, we hardly appreciate that this effective mental machinery is a comparatively recent discovery. When, again, some obstinate or newly discovered fact compels us to abandon one 'working hypothesis' which for a time has not only satisfied but served us, and construct another, and finally, after seesawing between observation and speculation, we experience the pleasure of extracting the truth, we have meanwhile run up an unpayable debt to the past.

The early Greeks were mainly deductive or *a priori* in their method. Aristotle, coming much later, after methods of thought had been studied, understood and taught induction almost as clearly as Bacon, but he mainly practised deduction. This was well, for in his period and during his lifetime, few steps in advance could have been made by the safer method, while he unquestionably promoted many great truths deductively. Giordano Bruno also recommended induction to others, but found it too tedious for his own purposes. While Bacon upheld induction in his writings as the true philosophical method, there is abundant evidence that it was already established as the method of scientific research by Harvey, who discovered the circulation of the blood, Mayo and others, quite independently and even in advance of Bacon; so it is not just that he should be credited with the revival of induction as applied to science during the seventeenth century; he was rather the first to formulate and teach it.

During the long Middle Ages, men had not observed Nature; they had studied Aristotle's views of Nature, and were anchored fast to Greek science by a traditional reverence. "*Bornons ce respect que nous avons pour les anciens*," said Pascal in his *Pensées*. This is also the vein of one of Bacon's Aphorisms: "Again, the reverence for antiquity and the authority of men who have been esteemed great in philosophy and general unanimity, have retarded men from advancing in science and almost enchanted them." Bacon also drew a satirical picture of the condition of natural science as it was early in the seventeenth century: "If the natural history extant, though apparently of great bulk and variety, were to be carefully weeded of its fables, antiquities, quotations, frivolous disputes, philosophy, ornaments, it would shrink to a slender bulk."

During the seventeenth and eighteenth centuries valuable materials were slowly gathering for the induction of Evolution. In the first revival of the idea the advances made were mainly deductive, yet each of the great philosophers of this period referred to one or more observations, and clearly aimed to establish a basis of fact for the mutability of species. This rational method spread so rapidly that a considerable part of the speculations of the naturalists Buffon and Erasmus Darwin, in the latter part of the seventeenth century, was directly based upon observation and was true interpretation. These were by far the most logical thinkers among the large number of eighteenth century evolutionists, who gave the imagination such free rein in support of the idea that Evolution and the 'working hypothesis' together fell into disrepute. A school that was professedly purely observational and inductive was established by Linnæus and Cuvier, and, owing to the genius of these naturalists, gained such ascendency that it was only after a bitter struggle in the early part of the nineteenth century, that the discredited working hypothesis acquired its true place as an instrument of thought. The evolutionists of the eighteenth and early part of the nineteenth century contended against great odds. They upheld a theory as to the origin of life which could not be established inductively in the existing state of knowledge, and which even at the time of the publication of the *Origin of Species* lacked verification. Although for the most part devout men, they were declared arch enemies of sound religion, and although right in their contention for the value of the inductive-deductive method of thought, they were also proclaimed as the enemies of sound scientific thinking.

THE ADVANCE OF NATURAL PHILOSOPHY.

The belief that the Bible contained a revelation of scientific as well as of spiritual and moral truths was not supported by the most prominent of the early theologians, nor many centuries later by Bacon. It is edifying to read the appeals of these two great Christian philosophers, Augustine and Bacon, for freedom of scientific thought, against the error of searching the Scriptures for laws of Nature.

"It very often happens," says Augustine, "that there is some question as to the earth or the sky, or the other elements of this world . . . respecting which one who is not a Christian has knowledge derived from most certain reasoning or observation" (that is, a scientific man), "and it is very disgraceful and mischievous and of all things to be carefully avoided, that a Christian speaking of such matters as being according to the Christian Scriptures, should be heard by an unbeliever talking such nonsense that the unbeliever perceiving him to be as wide from the mark as east from west, can hardly restrain himself from laughing."

Bacon (*Novum Organum*, Book I., Sec. 45), in his Aphorisms, deplores the corruption of Philosophy by the mixing up with it of superstition and theology, saying that it is most injurious both as a whole and in parts, and continues: —

"Against it we must use the greatest caution. . . . Yet some of the moderns have indulged this folly with such consummate inconsiderateness that they have endeavoured to build a system of Natural Philosophy on the First Chapter of Genesis, the Book of Job, and other parts of Scripture; seeking thus the dead amongst the living" (the interests of the soul). "And this folly is the more to be prevented and restrained, because not only fantastical philosophy but heretical religion spring from the absurd mixture of matters Divine and human. It is therefore most wise soberly to render unto faith the things that belong to faith." In the Introduction of *The Great Instauration*, he says: "For man, being a member and interpreter of Nature, acts and understands so far as he has observed of the order, the works, and the mind of Nature, and can proceed no further, for no power is able to loose or break the chain of causes, nor is Nature to be conquered but by submission."

A hard preliminary battle had to be fought by the philosophers for natural causation as against supernatural interference in the governing of the living world. Here lies the main debt of natural science to Philosophy; and to omit mention of the great names of the seventeenth and eighteenth centuries would leave a serious gap in these outlines. The natural philosophers of this time were more scientific than the professed scientists. They reached below metaphysics into questions which

to-day are left more exclusively to science. The
order of the Universe and the laws of Nature formed
a large part of speculation from the times of Bacon
to Schelling; in fact, now and again this speculation
sprang directly from observation of Nature, and it
is a most striking fact that every great philosopher
touched upon the Evolution idea. Bruno was a
radical evolutionist, although his notions were more
Oriental than European. Bacon foresaw the close
bearings of Variation and of experimental Evolution
upon species transformation. Descartes cautiously
advocated the Evolution idea. Leibnitz may even
be considered the head of a school of evolutionists.
Kant in his earlier writings held advanced views.
Thus the naturalists, whenever they passed from
direct observation to speculation upon the causes of
things, drew their suggestions and inspiration largely
from these philosophers.

This need not lead us into the history of the
discussion of primary causes, nor of the mechanical
and monistic *versus* the dualistic view of Nature.
The evolution of life as an organic law, more complex but comparable to any inorganic law, such as
gravitation, is one phase of natural causation. For
whatever principle regulates the rapid fall of a
wounded bird to the earth, is the same in kind, so
far as our philosophy of Nature is concerned, as
that which, during millions of years, has slowly
evolved the bird from the earth. Some of the
Greeks early saw this truth; yet in the progress

of later thought in Europe, the living world was the last to come under this principle of natural causation. The battle for it had to be first fought out in Cosmogony, then in Geology. So keen a philosopher as Kant believed that he saw two principles in Nature; one of natural causes reigning in lifeless matter, one of teleological causes reigning in living matter. This was because he could not conceive of any natural principle which could explain the beautiful adaptations and designs of Nature. From Geology the spread of the truth of natural causation reached the origin of the lower forms of life, and finally the origin of man. It is therefore a striking case of parallelism that the advance of our knowledge of development has repeated the actual cosmic order of development. Man first perceived Evolution in objects most remote, gradually in objects nearer to him, finally in himself.

Advance of Zoölogy and Botany.

The general state of knowledge of the different forms of life, next to the suggestiveness of Philosophy, was the most important factor in the environment of the Evolution idea, as food to the organism. The comparatively elementary knowledge of Aristotle rendered his speculations upon Evolution, at most, happy guesses at the truth. Embryology, Paleontology, Comparative Anatomy, and Distribution, the four pillars of modern Evolution, arose in the eighteenth century, but were not built into their scientific inductive form until the nineteenth century.

Yet the Greek traditions in natural history persisted as the environment of the Evolution idea as late as the end of the eighteenth century, and, as we shall see, the idea itself was framed solely upon Greek speculation. Most prominent among these Greek guesses at the truth was the doctrine of Abiogenesis, or *generatio æquivoca* — the spontaneous origin of life from lifeless matter. This fallacy exerted a most potent influence in shaping the crude theories of Evolution which were advanced during the seventeenth and eighteenth centuries; the absurdity of these theories reacting unfavourably upon the true Evolution idea by throwing it into discredit.

The accumulation of the natural evidences of Evolution was the work of centuries. Besides the advances in Astronomy, Geology, and Physical Geography, there was the slow upbuilding of the great branches of Biology. First, correct ideas of structure or Comparative Morphology of animals and plants, and connected with this the structure of extinct forms preserved as fossils; with this knowledge came the appreciation of the meaning of variations and of gradual development in structure, and the meaning of vestigial or degenerate structures. Then came the knowledge of function and the physiology, first of man, then of the lower animals; then the true ideas of individual development from the egg, or Embryology, connected with which many fallacies were current. Finally, Natural Environment began to be studied, or the relation of animals and plants to each other and to the surface of the globe, in connection with Distribution. In short, Evolution needed materials for induction. Unwilling Nature had to slowly yield up her secrets, and Evolution could not be conceived in its phyletic sense until all the knowledge embraced in Phylogeny had been more or less fully attained.

Let us first look at Structure. Anatomy had its infancy among the Greeks, and dissection was rudely practised. Aristotle was descended from a long race of physicians, yet his treatise on the structure of man is believed to show that he did not practise dissection. Scientific anatomy dates back to Galen, while modern anatomy began with the school of the University of Padua, where the human body was first fully dissected. In structure Aristotle observed the law of Analogy, as, for example, in his comparison of the functions of the fore and hind limbs. But the principle of Homology, or the fundamental likeness of type structure between the fore and hind limbs, was first pointed out by Vicq d'Azyr in 1805. Now Analogy is the Will-o'-the-wisp of Evolution; it is always leading us astray, as it did St. Hilaire in the third period, for functionally similar forms and forms with an external resemblance are produced over and over again in Nature, and do not always point to phyletic affinity, while Homology is one of our safest guides. The relations of organs to each other, or the idea that one structure is sacrificed for the development of another, now known as the law of *Economy of Growth*, was also perceived by Aristotle, but was first clearly stated by Goethe in 1807, and by St. Hilaire in 1818. Aristotle, following Democritus, was strongly impressed with the law of *Adaptation*, or the wonderful fitness of certain structures for certain ends, and Adaptation, with all its beautiful manifestations in Nature, has always been the focus of the differences between the Special Creationists and Evolutionists.

Degeneration, or the gradual decline of structures in form and usefulness, does not appear to have been perceived by Aristotle, although in his analysis of "Movement" he employs a very similar idea in connection with development. We first meet with Degeneration as part of an explanation of the origin of species, in the writings of Linnæus and Buffon in the eighteenth century; but the idea itself was much older, because we find it expressed in a passage of criticism of Sylvius upon Vesalius. Vesalius (1514–1564) had brought the charge against Galen (A.D. 131–200) that his work could not have been founded upon the human body, because he had described an intermaxillary bone. This bone, Vesalius observed, is found in the lower animals but not in man. Sylvius (1614-1672) defended Galen warmly, and argued that the fact that man had no intermaxillary bone at present was no proof that he did not have it in Galen's time. "It is luxury," he said, "it is sensuality which has gradually deprived man of this bone." This passage proves that the idea of degeneration of structure through disuse, as well as the idea of the inheritance of the effects of habit, or the 'transmission of acquired characters,' is a very ancient one.

Development, or increasing perfection of structure in course of Evolution, was the central thought of Aristotle's natural philosophy, but the term itself, as applied to the gradual increase in organs and single structures in the evolutionary sense, was first clearly used by Lamarck.

Embryological development was rightly conceived *a priori* by Aristotle in the form of Epigenesis, for he regarded the embryo as a mass of particles containing the potential capacity of development into the form of the adult. The term 'Evolution' was first introduced for the opposed embryological theory that the embryo contained the complete form in miniature, and that development consisted merely in the enlargement of this miniature. This doctrine of '*emboitement*' of Bonnet, defended by Swammerdam, Haller, Réaumur, and Cuvier, like the doctrine of Abiogenesis, long stood in the way of the progress of the Evolution idea; for if it were true that all beings had been preformed from the beginning, there could naturally be no evolution of form, nor any necessity for a theory of Evolution. Long before Aristotle, the principle of *Syngenesis*, or formation of the embryo by the union of elements from both parents, was rightly understood by Empedocles. The notion of *hereditary transmission* of characters was extremely ancient, and was naturally founded upon the early observed likeness of offspring to parents. Aristotle also commented upon the principles of the prepotency of the characteristics of one parent over the other, as well as of *Atavism*.

The growth of Embryology as an objective science came, of course, with the invention of microscopic lenses. Degraff, in the discovery of the ovum in 1678, Leeuwenhoek (1632-1723) in the discovery of the spermatozoön, laid the foundations of the science which Meckel, in 1813, and Von Baer, in 1827, built into one of the keystones of Evolution. Von Baer's law, that higher animals passed through embryonic stages in which they resemble the adult forms of lower types, was also dimly perceived by Aristotle, but not, of course, in its vital relation to Evolution.

Aristotle also distinguished between living and lifeless matter as the organic and inorganic, but in common with all the Greeks, and, in fact, with all zoölogists up to comparatively recent times, he believed in *Abiogenesis*, or the spontaneous development of living from lifeless matter. This belief was handed down through all the Middle Ages, and appeared in its crudest form as an explanation, not only of the origin of the lowest forms of life, but of the higher forms, even as late as the beginning of this century. As a spurious naturalistic explanation it was one of the greatest impediments to the growth of the true Evolution idea.

The law of *Biogenesis*, or of life from life, was clearly stated in Harvey's famous and oft-quoted dictum, *omne vivum ex ovo*, but was not finally demonstrated until quite late in the present century. The belief in spontaneous or direct origin from the earth thus began amongst the Greeks as an explanation of the origin of man and of the highest forms of life; it was gradually contracted to the origin of the lower and smaller forms of life, and finally, to the lowest invisible forms of bacteria, until, as an outcome of the discussions which are still fresh in our memory, between Pouchet and Pasteur in France, and Bastian and Tyndall in England, the theory of spontaneous origin of any form of life, even the lowest, was completely abandoned.

II.

AMONG THE GREEKS.

Die Gründer der griechischen Naturphilosophie im siebenten und sechsten Jahrhundert vor Christus waren es, die zuerst diesen wahren Grundstein der Erkenntniss legten und einen natürlichen gemeinsamen Urgrund aller Dinge zu erkennen suchten. — HAECKEL.

NEVER has the influence of Nature upon thought been more evident than in the philosophy and natural history of the Greeks. Whatever they may have drawn from the vague, abstract notions of development and transformation of Asiatic philosophers, they certainly recast into comparatively modern Evolutionism. No landlocked people could have put forth the rich suggestions of natural law which came from the long line of natural philosophers from Thales to Aristotle.

Their earliest known philosophy was a philosophy of Nature, of the origin and causes of the Universe. As Zeller observes, they aimed directly at a theory before considering the severe conditions required for the attainment of scientific knowledge. How, then, can we explain the nearness of their easy guesses at the secrets of Nature to the results of modern labor? Only through this influence of the '*milieu*,' of their physical surrounding upon their thought. It is in the environment of the sea we find the inspiration of Greek biological prophecy. Along the shores and in the waters of the blue Ægean, teeming with what we now know to be the earliest and simplest forms of animals and plants, they founded their hypotheses as to the origin and succession of life. Lucretius the Roman was Greek in spirit, but dwelling inland he substituted a terrestrial theory. Even the early Greek natural philosophy sprang more or less from observation, and therefore had some concrete value. It was not wholly imaginative.

The spirit of the Greeks was vigorous and hopeful. Not pausing to test their theories by research, they did not suffer the disappointments and delays which come from our own efforts to wrest truths from Nature. Combined with great freedom and wide range of ideas, independence of thought, and tendencies to rapid generalization, they had genuine gifts of scientific deduction, which enabled them to reach truth, as it were, by inspiration. As a case in point, Aristotle advanced a true theory of the nature of embryonic development by a very easy process, when contrasted with the slow steps which led to the establishment of the same theory of Epigenesis in the eighteenth century.

Their development from a childish to a mature philosophy was a slow one, and their thought upon Nature passed through four phases. First, the prehistoric mythological phase, which left its imprints in guesses as to the strange origin of monstrous forms of life, by the first natural philosophers who endeavoured to replace mythological by natural phenomena.

These pioneers contributed the spirit of the second phase, seen in the naturalism of the pre-Socratic period, suggesting Evolution, but neither conceiving of Evolution by slow stages of development nor seeking to explain Adaptation or Design in their systems of natural causation. They could not, in fact, speculate upon Design, as Zeller very acutely observes in reply to Lange, until the idea of Design as the result of a controlling Intelligence had arisen, and this idea was first developed by Anaxagoras, the last of the Physicists. He was followed by Socrates, who enlarged the theistic principle, which in the natural philosophy of Plato and in the natural history of Aristotle, inspired the third or teleological phase of thought. Then came the fourth phase, which was a naturalistic reaction to the novel and widely opposed mechanical or materialistic conceptions of the Universe developed by the Epicureans.

The Greek Periods. (*After Zeller.*)

GENERAL CONCEPTION OF NATURE.	DIVISIONS OF THE SCHOOLS.
Mythological.	The Prehistoric Traditions.
	I. *The Three Earliest Schools.*
FIRST PERIOD.	The Ionians. Thales (624–548), Anaximander (611–547), Anaximenes (588–524), Diogenes (440–).
Naturalistic.	The Pythagoreans. (580–430.)
	The Eleatics. Xenophanes (576–480), Parmenides (544–).
	II. *Physicists.*
Earlier *Materialistic.*	Heraclitus (535–475), Empedocles (495–435), Democritus (450–), Anaxagoras, (500–428).
SECOND PERIOD.	Socrates (470–399), Plato (427–347).
Teleological.	Aristotle (384–322).
	The Peripatetics, or post-Aristotelian school, including Theophrastus, Preaxagoras, Herophilus, Erasistratus.
THIRD PERIOD.	A. I. *The Stoics.*
Later Materialistic.	II. The Epicureans. Epicurus (341–270 B.C.).
	III. *The Sceptics.*
	B. I. *Eclecticism.* Galen (131–201 A.D.).

In Zeller's volumes on Greek Philosophy, and in his special discussion of Evolution among the Greeks, *Die Griechischen Vorgänger Darwin's*, we find a full examination of the speculations of these ancient philosophers. Lange and Haeckel tend to read into these speculations opinions which Zeller, with his more critical and exact analysis, throws into their actual relative value.

The Ionians and Eleatics.

THALES and ANAXIMANDER, the earliest Ionians, were students of Astronomy and of the origin of the Universe. So far as we know, they were the first who endeavoured to substitute a natural explanation of things for the old myths. Thales was also the first of the long line of natural philosophers who looked upon the great expanse of mother ocean and declared water to be the matter from which all things arose, and out of which they exist. This idea of the aquatic or marine origin of life, which is now a very widely accepted theory, is therefore an extremely ancient one. As has been said, it could only have arisen in a country surrounded by warm marine currents prodigal with shore and deep sea life.

ANAXIMANDER (611-547), the Milesian, is termed by Haeckel the prophet of Kant and Laplace in Cosmogony, and of Lamarck and Darwin in Biology! His theories were still largely imbued with mythology, and the more closely we examine them, the less they seem to resemble modern ideas. If we reduce this superlative prophetic mantle, we still find Anaximander imbued with a wealth of suggestion, and a literal prophet of some of the eighteenth century, rather than of the nineteenth century, speculations upon Evolution. He conceived of the earth as first existing in a fluid state. From its gradual drying up all living creatures were produced, *beginning with men.* These aquatic men first appeared in the form of fishes in the water, and they emerged from this element only after they had progressed so far as to be able to further develop and sustain themselves upon land. This is rather analogous to the bursting of a chrysalis, than to progressive development from a simpler to a more advanced structure by a change of organs, yet a germ of the Evolution idea is found here.

We find that Anaximander advanced some reasons for this view. He pointed to man's long helplessness after birth as one of the proofs that he cannot be in his original condition. His hypothetical ancestors of man were supposed to be first encased in horny capsules, floating and feeding in water; as soon as these 'fish-men' were in a condition to emerge, they came on land, the capsule burst, and they took their human form. Anaximander, naturally, is not staggered by the differences of internal organization necessary for aquatic or terrestrial life, nor are we to translate the word μεταβοῦν as 'adaptation' to new conditions of life, but simply as implying that the original fish-men persisted through their metamorphoses long enough to reproduce true men on land. There is, however, the dim notion here of survival or persistence throughout decidedly trying circumstances, which was greatly developed later by Empedocles. In the fragments of Anaximander's teachings we find he does not speculate upon the origin of other land animals, or intimate that he has any notion of the development of higher from lower organisms, except in the case of man. As to the origin of life in the beginning, he was the first teacher of the doctrine of Abiogenesis, believing that eels and other aquatic forms are directly produced from lifeless matter.

Grotesque as these ideas of Anaximander are, they indicate a marked advance over the autochthonous myths of earlier times, according to which man grew, like a plant, directly out of the earth; for we find here an attempt to explain human origin upon the basis of natural analogies. Unfortunately, so little knowledge of Anaximander's work is left us, that we can only obtain these vague glimpses of his opinions. ANAXIMENES, his pupil (588–524), found in air the cause of all things. Air, taking the form of the soul, imparts life, motion, and thought to animals. He introduced the idea of primordial terrestrial slime, a mixture of earth and water, from which, under the influence of the sun's heat, plants, animals, and human beings were directly produced — in the abiogenetic fashion. DIOGENES of Apollonia (440–   ), a 'late adherent of the Ionian school, also derived both plants and animals from this primordial earth slime. This is the prototype of Oken's *Ur-Schleim*.

XENOPHANES (576–480) was the founder of the Eleatic school, and is believed to have been a pupil of Anaximander. He agreed with his master so far as to trace the origin of man back to the transition period between the fluid or water and solid or land stages of the development of the earth, but we do not know how far he elaborated his ideas. The ultimate origin of life he traced to spontaneous generation, believing that the sun in warming the earth produces both animals and plants. He is famous in the annals of science as being the first to recognize fossils as remains of animals formerly alive, and to see in them the proofs that the seas formerly covered the earth, and that water was the element from which the earth emerged. PARMENIDES, his pupil, developed his cosmogony, and also derived men from the primitive earth slime directly engendered by the sun's heat.

THE PHYSICISTS.

The Physicists, Heraclitus, Empedocles, Democritus, and Anaxagoras, were far bolder and more fruitful in their suggestions. Among them we find that the vague notions of metamorphosis and the notions of Abiogenesis derived from the Ionians were developed into surprising anticipations of the true Evolution idea.

Heraclitus of Ephesus (535-475) gave the impetus to this advance. He was so profoundly impressed with the ceaseless revolutions in the Universe that he saw in *movement* the universal law. Everything was perpetually transposed into new shapes. It must not be supposed for a moment that Heraclitus had even a remote notion of the transformation process of life. He was rather a metaphysician than a natural philosopher; and his principal contribution to the Evolution idea was manifestly in his broad view of Nature, as involved in perpetual changes, yet always constituting a uniform whole.

Empedocles of Agrigentum (495-435) took a great stride beyond his predecessors, and may justly be called the father of the Evolution idea. He was not only a poet and musician, but made the first observations in Embryology which are recorded. Among his first physical principles we find the four elements — fire, air, water, and earth — played upon by two ultimate forces, a combining force, or love, and a separating force, or hate. He believed in Abiogenesis, or spontaneous generation, as the explanation of the origin of life, but that Nature does not produce the lower and higher forms simultaneously or without an effort. Plant life came first, and animal life developed only after a long series of trials. After the first formation of the earth, and before it was surrounded by the sun, plants arose, and from their budding forth came animals. But this origin he believed to be a very gradual process, for even now the living world presents a series of incomplete products. All organisms arose through the fortuitous play of the two great forces of Nature upon the four elements. Thus animals first appeared, not as complete individuals, but as parts of individuals, — heads without necks, arms without shoulders, eyes without their sockets. As a result of the triumph of love over hate, these parts began to seek each other and unite, but purely fortuitously. Thus out of this confused play of bodies, all kinds of accidental and extraordinary beings arose,—animals with the heads of men, and men with the heads of animals, even with double chests and heads like those of the guests in the Feast of Aristophanes. But these unnatural products soon became extinct, because they were not capable of propagation. Here it would appear that Empedocles was mainly endeavouring to give a naturalistic theory for the origin of the Centaurs, Chimæras, and other creations of Greek mythology. Thus, at least, Lucretius interpreted Empedocles many centuries later, putting these conjectures into verse (Book V. 860): —

> " Hence, doubtless, Earth prodigious forms at first
> Gendered, of face and members most grotesque :
> Monsters half-man, half-woman, not from each
> Distant, yet neither total ; shapes unsound,
> Footless and handless, void of mouth or eye,
> Or from misjunction, maimed, of limb with limb :

> To act all impotent, or flee from harm,
> Or nurture [1] take, their loathsome days t'extend.
>   These sprang at first and things alike uncouth ·
> Yet vainly; for abhorrent NATURE quick
> Checked their vile growths; . . .
>   Hence, doubtless, many a tribe has sunk supprest,
> Powerless its kind to gender.[2] For whate'er
> Feeds on the living ether, craft or speed,
> Or courage stern, from age to age preserves
> In ranks uninjured: . . .
>   Yet Centaurs lived not; nor could shapes like these
> Live ever, from two different natures reared,
> Discordant limbs and powers by powers reversed."

Empedocles imagined that after these unnatural products became extinct, other forms arose which were able to support themselves and multiply; but even these were not formed at once. First came shapeless masses built of earth and water, or earth slime, without limbs, organs of reproduction, or speech, thrown from fires beneath the earth. Later came the separation of the two sexes and the existing mode of reproduction. These trials of Nature were not a succession of organisms, improving as time went on, but a series of direct births from Nature, which were unfit to live, and hence eliminated, until, after ceaseless trials, Nature produced the fit and perpetual tribes.

Thus, in the ancient teachings of Empedocles, we find the germ of the theory of the *Survival*

[1-2] It is interesting to note the remote parallel with the modern notion of the 'struggle for existence' as, mainly, success in feeding and in leaving progeny.

of the Fittest, or of Natural Selection. And the absolute proof that Empedocles' crude hypothesis embodied this world famous thought, is found in passages in Aristotle's *Physics*, in which he refers to Empedocles as having first shown the possibility of the origin of the fittest forms of life through chance rather than through Design. With Empedocles himself, however, it was no more than the potential germ of suggestion, which, in the brilliant mind of Aristotle, was stated precisely in its modern form, as we shall see later in our study of Aristotle.

Lange attributes to Democritus a similar interpretation of Empedocles' teaching, namely, the "attainment of adaptations through the infinitely repeated play of production and annihilation, in which finally that alone survives which bears the guarantee of persistence through its relatively fortuitous constitution." But Zeller takes a more conservative and sounder view of the real meaning of this old philosopher of Agrigentum. He says this could not have been advanced by Empedocles as an explanation of Design in Nature, because this idea had not yet been formulated in the Greek mind.

Empedocles was an evolutionist only in so far as he taught the gradual substitution of the less by the more perfect forms of life. He had a dim adumbration of the truth. There is no glimmering of slow development through the successive modification of lower into higher forms. His beings, which were incapable of feeding, reproducing, or defending themselves, were all produced spontaneously, or directly from the earth. He thus simply modified the abiogenetic hypothesis, and, by happy conjecture, gave his theory a semblance of modern Evolution, with four sparks of truth, — first, that the development of life was a gradual process; second, that plants were evolved before animals; third, that imperfect forms were gradually replaced (not succeeded) by perfect forms; fourth, that the natural cause of the production of perfect forms was the extinction of the imperfect.

DEMOCRITUS (450– B.C.), the founder of the Atomistic philosophy, and precursor of materialism, studied and compared the principal organs of man and the lower animals. Cuvier has called him the first comparative anatomist. He did not, as Zeller points out, further the Evolution idea, because his teaching was not constructive in the way of advancing explanations of natural phenomena; it was simply destructive as regards Teleology. He perceived Design and admired the adaptations of Nature, but left their origin unexplained. As Zeller observes, Democritus had a gift for observing the purposeful direction and the functions of bodily organs, and was in every way inclined, one would think, to explain these adaptations upon the principles of his mechanical philosophy, for he stood far from a teleological conception of Nature, yet he advanced no explanations. He denied that the Universe was created or ordered by reason. He adopted the older views as to the origin of animals and plants directly from the terrestrial slime. His main indirect contribution to the sub-structure of Evolution was his perception of the principle of the *adaptation of single structures and organs* to certain purposes, — an important step in advance, for Empedocles' notion of adaptation extended only to organisms as a whole.

ANAXAGORAS (500–428 B.C.) took a further step. According to Plato and Aristotle, this philosopher was the first to attribute adaptations in Nature to Intelligent Design, and was thus the founder of Teleology. He also was the first to trace the origin of animals and plants to pre-existing germs in the air and ether. That the idea of Design was only developed in his mind to a very limited extent is shown in his history of the Universe. All things existed, in some form, from the beginning. There were the germs, seeds, or miniatures of plants, animals, and minerals intermingled in the mass of matter. These germs had to be separated from the mass and arranged under the direction of Mind or Reason. The original chaos was heated; it divided into cold mist and warm ether. Water, earth, and minerals were formed from the former. The germs of plants were floating in the air; then they were carried down by the rains, and produced vegetation. The germs of animals, including those of man, were in the ether; they were fructified by the warm and moist terrestrial slime. In regard to Anaxagoras' conception of adaptations as due to intelligent design in Nature, Zeller says: —

> "The question whether the purposefulness of the tendencies of Nature (Natureinrichtung) could be explained without a purposeful working natural force — this question could not be raised until men had observed adaptation in Nature and had begun to attribute it to Intelligent Design. No one, according to Aristotle and Plato, had taken this step before *Anaxagoras*. But even he applied this newly discovered principle in exceptional cases, — not to the origin of life, surely, for he derived plants and animals from the air and ether. He did not, therefore, further the explanation of the problem of design in Nature, which Empedocles is mistakenly supposed to have raised."

ARISTOTLE.

> Give me no peeping scientist, if I
> Shall judge God's grandly-ordered world aright;
> But give, to plant my Cosmic survey high,
> The wisest of wise Greeks, the Stagirite.
> — JOHN STUART BLACKIE.

With ARISTOTLE (384–322) we enter a new world. He towered above his predecessors, and by the force of his own genius created Natural History. In his own words, lately quoted by Romanes, we learn that the centuries preceding him yielded him nothing but vague speculation: —

> "I found no basis prepared; no models to copy. . . . Mine is the first step, and therefore a small one, though worked out with much thought and hard labor. It must be looked at as a first step and judged with indulgence. You, my readers, or hearers of my lectures, if you think I have done as much as can fairly be

required for an initiatory start, as compared with more advanced departments of theory, will acknowledge what I have achieved and pardon what I have left for others to accomplish."

In the *Physics* and in the *Natural History of Animals*, are contained Aristotle's views of Nature and his remarkable observations upon the plant and animal kingdoms. He was thoroughly versed in old Greek philosophy, and begins many of his treatises with a history of opinion, after the modern German fashion. He frequently quotes and discusses the opinions of Empedocles, Parmenides, Democritus, Heraclitus, Anaxagoras, and others. He undoubtedly inherited his taste for science from the line of physicians upon his father's side, perhaps from the Asclepiads, who are said to have practised dissection. He was attracted to natural history by his boyhood life upon the seashore, and the main parts of his ideas upon Evolution were evidently drawn from his own observations upon the gradations between marine plants and the lower and higher forms of marine animals. He was the first to conceive of a genetic series, and his conception of a single chain of evolution from the polyps to man was never fully replaced until the beginning of this century. It appeared over and over again in different guises. In all his philosophy of Nature, Aristotle was guided partly by his preconceived opinions derived from Plato and Socrates, and partly by convictions derived from his own observations upon the wonderful order and perfection of the Universe. His 'perfecting principle' in Nature is only one of a score of his legacies to later speculation upon Evolution causation. Many of our later writers are Aristotelians without apparently being conscious of it.

Let us first look at Aristotle's equipment as a naturalist. He enters a plea for the study and dissection of lower types: " Hence we ought not with puerile fastidiousness to neglect the contemplation of more ignoble animals; for in all animals there is something to admire because in all there is the natural and the beautiful." He distinguished five hundred species of mammals, birds, and fishes, besides exhibiting an extensive knowledge of polyps, sponges, cuttlefish, and other marine forms of life. His four essays upon the parts, locomotion, generation, and vital principle of animals, show that he fully understood Adaptation in its modern sense; he recognized the analogies if not the homologies between different organs like the limbs; he distinguished between the homogeneous tissues made up of like parts and the heterogeneous organs made up of unlike parts; he perceived the underlying principle of physiological division of labour in the different organs of the body; he perceived the unity of plan or type in certain classes of animals, and considered rudimentary organs as tokens whereby Nature sustains this unity; he rightly conceived of life as the function of the organism, not as a separate principle; he anticipated Harvey's doctrine of Epigenesis in embryonic development; he fully perceived the forces of hereditary transmission, of the prepotency of one parent or stock, and of Atavism or Reversion; he also perceived the 'compensation of growth' principle as shown in a passage of his upon the origin of horns: "Having now explained the purpose of horns, it remains to see the necessity of matter, by which Nature gave horns to animals; we see that Nature taking away matter from the front teeth (alluding to the ruminants) has added it to the horns." He saw the fundamental difference between animals and plants, and distinguished the organic or living world from the inorganic or lifeless world.

In his treatise upon the *Generation of Animals* (I. Sec. 35) we find him discussing the Heredity theories of Hippocrates and Heraclitus, which were similar to those of Democritus, and to the later Pangenesis of Darwin. He says:—

"Children resemble their parents not only in congenital characters, but in those acquired later in life. For cases are known where parents have been marked by scars, and children have shown traces of these scars at the same points; a case is also reported from Chalcedon in which a father had been branded with a letter, and the same letter somewhat blurred and not sharply defined appeared upon the arm of his child."

Aristotle, however, does not accept the Pangenesis hypothesis of Heredity, nor does he suggest the inheritance of normal functional modifications. In his *History of Animals* he again refers to the inheritance of mutilations, remarking that such inheritance, although observed, is decidedly rare.[1]

We can pass leniently by errors which are strewn among such grand contributions to Biology and to the very foundation-stones of the Evolution idea. Aristotle showed practical ignorance of human anatomy and physiology; he failed to establish a natural classification; he also fostered the abiogenetic myth, that not only smaller but larger animals, such as frogs, snakes, and eels, are produced spontaneously from the mud. Some of these and many other of his mistaken teachings were not wholly outlived until the present century; yet we may not allow them to detract from our general admiration of his great genius. His failures in descriptive science were chiefly in statements where he departed from his own principle of verification, and relied upon the scientific hearsay of his day.

Aristotle's method has been fully discussed in Lewes' very interesting work, *Aristotle: a Chapter in the History of Science.* While Plato had relied upon intuitions as the main ground of true knowledge, Aristotle relied upon experiment and induction. "We must not," he said, "accept a general principle from logic only, but must prove its application to each fact; for it is in facts that we must seek general principles, and these must always accord with facts. Experience furnishes the partic-

[1] See Brock, "Einige ältere Autoren über die Vererbung erworbener Eigenschaften." Biolog. Centralbl. VIII. p. 491.

ular facts from which induction is the pathway to general laws" (*History of Animals*, I. 6). He held that errors do not arise because the senses are false media, but because we put false interpretations upon their testimony.

Aristotle's theories as to the origin and succession of life went far beyond what he could have reached by the legitimate application of his professed method of procedure. Having now briefly considered the materials of his knowledge, let us carefully examine how he put his facts together into an Evolution system which had the teachings of Plato and Socrates for its primary philosophical basis.

Aristotle believed in a complete gradation in Nature, a progressive development corresponding with the progressive life of the soul. Nature, he says, proceeds constantly by the aid of gradual transitions from the most imperfect to the most perfect, while the numerous analogies which we find in the various parts of the animal scale show that all is governed by the same laws, — in other words, Nature is a unit as to its causation. The lowest stage is the inorganic, and this passes into the organic by direct metamorphosis, matter being transformed into life. Plants are animate as compared with minerals, and inanimate as compared with animals; they have powers of nourishment and reproduction, but no feeling or sensibility. Then come the plant-animals, or Zoöphytes; these are the marine creatures, such as sponges and sea-anemones, which leave the observer most in doubt, for they grow upon rocks and die if detached. (Polyps Aristotle wrongly thought were plants, while sponges he rightly considered animals.) The third step taken by Nature is the development of animals with sensibility,— hence desire for food and other needs of life, and hence locomotion to fulfil these desires. Here was a more complex and energetic form of the original life. Man is the highest point of one long and continuous ascent; other animals have the faculty of thought; man alone generalizes and forms abstractions; he is physically superior in his erect position, in his purest and largest blood supply, largest brain, and highest temperature.

How was this progression effected?

Here we come to the second feature in Aristotle's theory, which is more or less metaphysical,— it is the idea of the development of the potentiality of perfection into actuality, the creation of *form* in *matter*. " Nature does nothing without an aim." "She is always striving after the most beautiful that is possible.' Aristotle perceived a most marvellous adaptation in the arrangement of the world, and felt compelled to assume Intelligent Design as the primary cause of things, by the perfection and regularity which he observed in Nature. Nothing, he held, which occurs regularly can be the result of accident. This perfection is the outcome of an all-pervading *movement*, which we should, in nineteenth-century language, speak of as an 'internal perfecting tendency.' In Aristotle's conception of 'movement,' as outlined in his *Physics*, we find something very analogous to our modern biological conception of transformation in development, for he analyzes 'movement' as every change, as every realization of what is possible, consisting in': (*a*) *Substantial* movement, origin and decay, as we should now say, development and degeneration; (*b*) *Quantitative* movement, addition and subtraction, or, in modern terms, the gain and loss of parts; (*c*) *Qualitative* movement, or the transition of one material into another, in metamorphosis and change of function; (*d*) *Local* movement, or change of place, in the transposition of parts.

Thus Aristotle thought out the four essential features of Evolution as a process; but we have found no evidence that he actually applied this conception to the development of organisms or of organs, as we do now in the light of our modern knowledge of the actual stages of Evolution. This enables us to understand Aristotle's view of Nature as the principle of motion and rest comprised in his four Causes. Here again he is more or less metaphysical. The first is the 'physical Material cause,' or matter itself; the second is the 'physical Formal cause,' or the forces of the 'perfecting principle'; the third is the 'abstract Final cause,' the fitness, adaptation, or purpose, the good of each and all; the fourth, presiding over all, is the 'Efficient cause,' the Prime Mover, or God. Aristotle attributed all the imperfections of Nature to the struggle between the material and formal causes,— to the resistance of matter to form. There is room for difference of opinion as to whether he considered the Efficient cause, or God, as constantly present and working in Nature, or as having established a preordained harmony. Romanes points out that Aristotle, in his *Metaphysics*, asks the question whether the principle of order and excellence is self-existing from the beginning (*i.e.* the operation of natural laws), or whether, like the discipline of an army, it is apparently inherent, but really due to a general in the background.

Whether or not Aristotle viewed the Prime Mover as sustaining his laws or as having preordained them, he certainly does not believe in Special Creation, either of adaptations or of organisms, nor in the interference of the Prime Mover in Nature; the struggle towards perfection is a natural process, as where he says: "It is due to the resistance of matter to form that Nature can only rise by degrees from lower to higher types." There is, therefore, no doubt that he was not a teleologist in the ordinary sense; at the very heart of his theory of Evolution was this 'internal perfecting tendency,' driving organisms progressively forward into more perfect types. He viewed man as the flower of

Nature, towards which all had been tending, the crowning end, purpose, or final cause. His theory was then anthropocentric: "plants are evidently for the sake of animals and animals for the sake of man; thus Nature, which does nothing in vain, has done all things for the sake of man."

Aristotle's view is brought out clearly and emphatically in the most striking passage of all his writings where he undertakes to refute Empedocles. This is of the greatest interest to-day, because Aristotle clearly states and rejects a theory of the origin or adaptive structures in animals altogether similar to that of Darwin. Aristotle perceived in Empedocles' crude suggestion of the survival of adapted and extinction of inadapted beings, the gist of an argument which might be applied not only to entire organisms but to parts of organisms, to explain purposive structures, and which might thus become a dangerous rival to his own theory of the origin of purposive structures by the direct operation of his 'perfecting principle.' In the following passages, selected from the early books of his *Physics*, we seem to gain a clear insight into Aristotle's whole chain of reasoning, in a manner which enables us to compare it with modern lines of thought. The headings and parentheses are my own; the passages are selected and adapted from Taylor's translation of the *Physics* and brought together to give a clear idea of Aristotle's meaning in his own language.

a. *Nature is twofold, namely, Form and Matter.*

For if we look to the ancient philosophers, such as Empedocles and Democritus, it would seem that matter alone should be regarded, for they attended in a very small degree to form . . . . but it is the province of physical science to have a knowledge of both. Further, it belongs to physical science to consider the purpose or end for which a thing subsists. The poet was led to say: —

"An end it has, for which it was produced."

This is absurd, for not that which is last deserves the name of end, but that which is most perfect.

b. *Of Fortuity in Nature.*

Empedocles[1] says that the greater part of the members of animals were generated by chance; while there are others who assign chance as the cause of the heavenly bodies, and Intellect (or Design) as the cause of all earthly bodies. But it is more probable that the heavens should have been produced by Nature, Intellect (Design), or something else of this kind, and that they should exist through such a designing cause than that frail and mortal animals were produced by it; for order and a firm and cer-

[1] Empedocles does not speak rightly when he says that many things are inherent in animals because it thus happened in their generation; as for instance a spine composed of many vertebræ not produced for some purpose, but from chance or accident. (*Parts of Animals*, Book I.)

tain constitution or being are far more obvious in celestial natures than in us; but an uncertain, inconstant, and fortuitous condition is rather the property of the mortal race. . . . Chance and fortune are sequels (secondary) to both Intellect and Nature. Hence if chance were in an eminent degree the cause of the heavens, it would nevertheless be necessary that Intellect and Nature should be prior causes of many other things as well as of this Universe itself.

c. *Of Necessity (Law) and Design in Nature.*

We must show first, why Nature is a cause which subsists for some *purpose*, and second, how *necessity* (Natural law) subsists in physical concerns, for all natural causes are referred to this. But some may question what hinders Nature from operating for some purpose rather than from necessity; for example, that rain falls for the benefit of the corn rather than because that ascending vapour must be cooled and cooling it must descend as water. But Jupiter rains not that corn may be increased, but from necessity. Similarly, if some one's corn is destroyed by rain, it does not rain for this purpose, but as an accidental circumstance. It does not appear to be from fortune or chance that it frequently rains in winter, but from necessity (law).

d. *Adaptive Structures not Produced by Survivals of the Fittest.*

What, then, hinders but that the parts in Nature may also thus arise (namely, according to law). For instance, that the teeth should arise from necessity, the front teeth sharp and adapted to divide the food, the grinders broad and adapted to breaking the food into pieces.

(Another explanation may be offered.) Yet, it may be said that they were not made for this purpose (*i.e.* for this adaptation), but that this (adaptative) purposive arrangement came about by chance; and the same reasoning is applied to other parts of the body in which existence for some purpose is apparent. And *it is argued that where all things happened as if they were made for some purpose, being aptly (adaptively) united by chance, these were preserved, but such as were not aptly (adaptively) made, these were lost and still perish*, according to what Empedocles says concerning the bull species with human heads. This, therefore, and similar reasoning, may lead some to doubt on this subject.

It is, however, impossible that these (adaptive) parts should subsist (arise) in this manner; for these parts, and everything which is produced in Nature, are either always, or, for the most part, thus (*i.e.* adaptively) produced; and this is not the case with anything which is produced by fortune or chance,[1] even as it does not appear to be fortune or chance that it frequently rains in winter. . . . If these things appear to be either by chance, or to be for some purpose, — and we have shown that they cannot be by chance, — then it follows that they must be for some purpose. There is, therefore, a purpose in things which are produced by, and exist from, Nature.

e. *A Sequence of Purposive Productions.*

Since, also, Nature is twofold, consisting of matter and of form, the latter being an end for the sake of which the rest subsists, form will also be a cause for the sake of which natural productions subsist. . . . *Further still, it is necessary* (i.e. *according to law*) *that germs should have been first produced, and not immediately animals; and that soft mass which first subsisted was the germ.* In plants, also, there is purpose, but it is less distinct; and this shows that plants were produced in the same manner as animals, not by chance, as by the union of olives upon grape vines. Similarly, it may be argued, that there should be an accidental generation (or production) of the germs of things, but he who asserts this subverts Nature herself, for Nature produces those things which, being *continually moved by a certain principle contained in themselves,* arrive at a certain end.

[1] Compare Darwin: "I have spoken of variations sometimes as if they were due to chance. This is a wholly incorrect expression; it merely serves to acknowledge plainly our ignorance of the cause of each particular variation."

These passages seem to contain absolute evidence that Aristotle had substantially the modern conception of the Evolution of life, from a primordial, soft mass of living matter to the most perfect forms, and that even in these he believed Evolution was incomplete for they were progressing to higher forms. His argument of the analogy between the operation of natural law, rather than of chance, in the lifeless and in the living world; is a perfectly logical one, and his consequent rejection of the hypothesis of the Survival of the Fittest, a sound induction from his own limited knowledge of Nature. It seems perfectly clear that he placed all under secondary natural laws. If he had accepted Empedocles' hypothesis, he would have been the literal prophet of Darwinism.

The Post-Aristotelians.

Thus, in this great natural philosopher, we reach the highest level attained by the Greeks, and we now pass to a rapid decline in Greek productiveness until its final extinction. We notice a marked chasm between his theistic, or dualistic, teaching and the sceptical, or rather agnostic, and, to a certain extent, monistic, teaching of Epicurus. This gap widened. The materialistic and agnostic tendency of Empedocles, Democritus, and Epicurus was revived by Lucretius, and culminated in him for the time. The theistic tendency of Aristotle led to his adoption by, and great influence with, the philosophers of the early Christian Church. In general, the movement of free physical inquiry among the Greeks was checked by the conquest of Alexander and the loss of national independence. The interest in investigation into Nature, and speculation upon the causes of things, subsided. Ethics rose among the Stoics. The Epicureans developed a mechanical and anti-teleological conception of the Universe, but they did not advance the inquiry into natural causation.

Aristotle's scientific teachings were continued by his pupils among the Peripatetics, Theophrastus and Preaxagoras, and their successors, Herophilus and Erasistratus. Unfortunately, the greater part of the works of Theophrastus, who was both botanist and mineralogist, are lost; his *History of Plants* was an attempt to supplement the *History of Animals* of his master. The last two members of this school were physicians, who continued their studies in Alexandria and became the most distinguished human anatomists of the time before Galen.

PLINY (A.D. 23-79), the Roman, the next naturalist of note, was rather a collector of anecdotes than an observer. The last of the Greek naturalists were Dioscoridus, a physician, observer, and botanist living in the time of the Cæsars, and the celebrated Galen, physician and anatomist, living under Marcus Aurelius. Galen (131-200) has been compared both with Hippocrates (B.C. 460-377) and with Aristotle, whose method of observation he followed and applied to human anatomy. This was the waning of the scientific movement under Grecian influence.

Let us now return to the successors of Democritus. The only writer of the Third or Post-Aristotelian Period of Greek Philosophy who concerns us here is Epicurus.

EPICURUS' (341-270) chief interest in philosophy was to establish the principle of natural *versus* that of supernatural causation. He originated nothing in Evolution, but gathered from Empedocles and Democritus arguments in support of the principle of natural law. Zeller observes as his characteristic that he was totally lacking in the scientific spirit which could qualify him as an investigator. His main animus was to combat the supernatural from every side, yet he was unable to direct his followers to any naturalistic explanation of value, giving them rather free rein in the choice of the most groundless hypotheses. As for the general conception that the purposeful could arise by selection or survival from the unpurposeful, which is credited to Epicureanism by some modern writers, this conception belongs primarily to Aristotle, who, as we have seen, formulated the crude myth of Empedocles into the language of modern science, with the motive of clearly stating a possible explanation of the origin of the purposeful in order to clearly refute it. Epicurus was influenced by Democritus and his doctrine of Atomism, excluding Teleology at every present point as well as at the beginning of the world, supporting the mechanical conception of Nature, and maintaining that every individual thing is to be explained in a purely mechanical manner. Convinced that only natural causes prevail, Epicurus did not concern himself with inquiries as to their character. He also taught the origin of life by spontaneous generation, that living beings arose directly from the earth, including many marvellous forms, and adopted Empedocles' notion, that only those capable of life and reproduction have been preserved.

From Epicurus we take a long leap in time to T. Lucretius Carus, the Roman poet, whose inquiry into the origin and nature of living things, as we have observed, revived the teachings of Empedocles, of Democritus, and especially of Epicurus. He connected with these many observations of his own. The fact that he was an original observer of Nature must be inferred from his considerable knowledge of animals and plants. It is possible that the observations treated in his great poem may have been more precisely recorded in some of his lost books.

LUCRETIUS (99–55) was the second poet of Evolution. His *De Rerum Natura* resuscitated the doctrines of Epicurus, and set them in a far more favourable light, building up anew the mechanical conception of Nature. Lucretius was also familiar with Empedocles, and, as we have seen, puts his teachings in verse. Here, again, is a difference of opinion between Lange and Zeller. Lange refers to the end of the first book, in which he claims that Lucretius briefly announces the magnificent doctrine first proposed by Empedocles, that all the adaptations to be found in the Universe, and especially in organic life, are merely special cases of the infinite possibilities of mechanical events. Thus Lucretius says : —

"For verily not by design do the first beginnings of things station themselves each in his right place, occupied by keen-sighted intelligence, . . . but because after trying motions and unions of every kind, at length they fall into arrangements, such as those out of which this our sum of things has been formed, . . . and the earth, fostered by the heat of the sun, begins to renew this produce, and the race of living things to come up and flourish."

Zeller rightly contends that Lucretius did not really apply the Empedocles theory to the origin of adaptations as in the modern Darwinian sense; for his treatment is simply a poetical restatement of Empedocles' own words, unmodified by the great advances of science. The creations which, according to Lucretius, were thus eliminated from the earth were the mythical monsters, such as the Centaurs and the Chimæras.

Lucretius places the mechanical conception of Nature over against the teleological; we find that he does not carry his conception of Nature as Aristotle does into the law of gradual development of organic life, but like Parmenides, Democritus, and Anaxagoras, he conceives of animals as arising directly from the earth: " Plants and trees," he says (Book V. 780), "arise directly out of the earth in the same manner that feathers and hair grow from the bodies of animals. Living beings certainly have not fallen down from heaven, nor, as Anaxagoras supposed, have land animals arisen from the sea. But as even now many animals under the influence of rain, and the heat of the sun, arise from the earth, so under the fresh, youthful, productive forces of the younger earth, they were spontaneously produced in larger numbers. In this manner were first produced birds, from the warmth of spring; then other animals sprang from the womb of the earth, since first mounds grew up from which people sprang forth, for they had been nourished within. In an analogous manner these young earth-children were nourished by springs of milk."

Only as an after-thought, not as a part of Nature's method, Lucretius borrows from Epicurus, and thus probably indirectly from Empedocles, the Survival of the Fittest idea that some of these earth-born beings were unable to live, and were replaced by others. As a rationalist, he naturally suppressed the mythological Centaur and Chimæra from his direct history of Creation. In the following passages we find these purely fanciful speculations of Lucretius beautifully expressed: —

> "And first the race she reared of verdant herbs,
> Glistening o'er every hill; the fields at large
> Shone with the verdant tincture, and the trees
> Felt the deep impulse, and with outstretched arms
> Broke from their bonds rejoicing. As the down
> Shoots from the winged nations, or from beasts
> Bristles or hair, so poured the new-born earth
> Plants, fruits, and herbage. Then, in order next,
> Raised she the sentient tribes, in various modes,
> By various powers distinguished: for nor heaven
> Down dropped them, nor from ocean's briny waves
> Sprang they, terrestrial sole; whence, justly, EARTH
> Claims the dear name of mother, since alone
> Flowed from herself whate'er the sight surveys.
>
> E'en now oft rears she many a sentient tribe,
> By showers and sunshine ushered into day.
> Whence less stupendous tribes should then have risen
> More, and of ampler make, herself new-formed,
> In flower of youth, and ETHER all mature.
>
> Of these birds first, of wing and plume diverse,
> Broke their light shells in springtime: as in spring
> Still breaks the grasshopper his curious web,
> And seeks, spontaneous, foods and vital air.
>
> . . . .
>
> Hence the dear name of mother, o'er and o'er,
> Earth claims most justly, since the race of man
> Long bore she of herself, each brutal tribe
> Wild-wandering o'er the mountains, and the birds
> Gay-winged, that cleave, diverse, the liquid air."

It thus appears that we cannot truly speak of Lucretius as an evolutionist, in the sense of gradual development by descent, although he believed in the successive appearance of different forms of life. His nearest approach to true Evolution teaching was in his account of the development of the faculties and arts among the races of men. In shutting out Aristotle and his view of Nature, he excluded the only Greek who came near the modern idea of descent of higher forms from lower. The animals and plants of Lucretius arise full-formed direct from the earth. This is not Evolution, yet it plays an important part in the later history of the idea. Views not unlike these were revived as late as the eighteenth century.

Although a Roman, Lucretius was virtually a Greek in his natural philosophy. He terminated a period of thought, and in his poem summed up all the non-Aristotelian teachings in a pure form. After him the Greek ideas were grafted upon Arabic and Christian philosophy and science. This is, therefore, the point at which to consider what were the Greek legacies to their followers.

The Legacy of the Greeks.

The first element in the legacy of the Greeks was their scientific curiosity, their desire to find a natural explanation for the origin and existence of things. This is by no means a universal characteristic of the human mind, for we know that many Eastern races are wholly devoid of it, and have made no scientific progress. The ground motive in science is a high order of curiosity, led on by ambition to overcome obstacles.

The first biological question asked by the Greeks was as to the origin of life; and extremely early arose the doctrine of Anaximander, that all life originated in spontaneous generation from the water. Later this was somewhat modified into the doctrine that life originated in the primordial terrestrial slime, or mingling of earth and water, especially along the emerging shores of the earth. This was held by Empedocles. Later still, quite a distinct idea was put forth by Anaxagoras, that life originated in the coming together and development of pre-existent germs in the air or ether, animals and plants springing directly from them. This origin of life from germs, of course surreptitiously placed the problem only one degree further back, apparently, but not really evading the difficulty. It was a fruitful idea, and thereafter many of the doctrines as to the origin of life contained the conception of primordial germs. Aristotle came nearest the modern conception of protozoan primordial life when he wrote that all animals and plants originated in germs composed of soft masses of matter, although he inconsistently taught that even some of the higher forms sprang directly from the earth, leaving out the germ stage altogether.

The real Evolution idea among the Greeks had its roots in the notion of the changing rather than of the fixed order of things, which came from

Heraclitus. The essence of this principle, that everything was in a state of movement, and nothing had reached a state of rest, underlies the later doctrine of the gradually increasing perfection of organisms. The essence of the idea of the gradual development of organisms, however, was much earlier, for it originated with Anaximander, upon whose rude notion of the origin of the 'fish-men' Empedocles and other writers built up their theories. Empedocles added to the conception of development a number of important principles. First, he suggested that plant life preceded animal life, and this suggestion was taken up and expanded by Aristotle. Second, he concluded that the present world of life was still formative or incomplete, a modification of the general notion of Heraclitus. Third, he suggested, with apparently remarkable prevision, that the first organisms were formless masses without distinctions of sex, that afterwards the sexes were separated, and that the existing modes of reproduction of the less perfect were followed by the more perfect. This idea, as we have seen, however, was not even remotely related to our modern conception of primordial asexual organisms, for his 'formless masses' were mythological monsters.

Empedocles further set forth a rude doctrine of the successive production directly from the earth of larger animal types possessing greater or lesser capacity of living and reproducing. The less perfect forms, as well as the more perfect, were produced fortuitously. The misshapen, ill-combined monsters were eliminated, one after the other, until finally Nature produced animals capable of feeding themselves and of propagation. Aristotle developed a wholly different notion of successive development, more like the modern theory in the succession of higher organisms from lower by descent and modification.

Together with these vague conceptions of the fact of the gradual Evolution of life, was associated as a theoretical explanation, first, the dimly foreshadowed 'Survival of the Fittest' theory of Empedocles, that the perfect forms were finally produced as the result of a long series of fortuitous combinations, and the wholly diverse theory of Aristotle that there was no fortuity in Evolution, but that the succession of forms was due to the action of an internal perfecting principle originally implanted by the Divine Intelligence.

Finally, the principles of Adaptation, or fitness of certain structures to certain ends, had been clearly brought out, and gave rise to the distinct problem of the origin or cause of adaptations. So that we can find in Aristotle, most clearly stated, the great question which has been one of the burning questions of Biology ever since — Whether or not adaptations are due solely to the fortuitous combination of parts?

Thus the Greeks left the later world face to face

with the problem of Causation in three forms: first, whether Intelligent Design is constantly operating in Nature; second, whether Nature is under the operation of natural causes originally implanted by Intelligent Design; and third, whether Nature is under the operation of natural causes due from the beginning to the laws of chance, and containing no evidences of design, even in their origin.

III.

THE THEOLOGIANS AND NATURAL PHILOSOPHERS.

Eine höchst wichtige Betrachtung der Geschichte der Wissenschaften ist die, dass sich aus den ersten Anfängen einer Entdeckung manches in den Gang des Wissens heran- und durchzieht, welches den Fortschritt hindert, sogar öfters lähmt. — GOETHE.

As all learning in Europe was for centuries under the guardianship of the Church, it is important to look into the teachings of the great theologians upon the origin and development of life. This teaching sprang from two sources, — the revelation of the order of Creation in the Book of Genesis, and the natural philosophy of Plato and Aristotle.

Philo of Alexandria introduced in the first century what has been described as the 'Hellenizing of the Old Testament,' or the allegorical method of exegesis. By this, as Erdmann observes, the Bible narrative was found to contain a deeper, and particularly an allegorical, in addition to its literal, interpretation; this was not conscious disingenuousness but a natural mode of amalgamating the Greek philosophic with the Hebraic doctrines.

Among the Christian Fathers the movement towards a partly naturalistic interpretation of the order of Creation was made by Gregory of Nyssa in the fourth century, and was completed by Augustine in the fourth and fifth centuries. Plainly as the direct or instantaneous Creation of animals and plants appeared to be taught in Genesis, Augustine read this in the light of primary causation and the gradual development from the imperfect to the perfect of Aristotle.

This most influential teacher thus handed down to his followers opinions which closely conform to the progressive views of those theologians of the present day who have accepted the Evolution theory. In proof of this Greek influence we find that Augustine also adopted some of the Greek notions of the spontaneous generation of life. In the Middle Ages analogous views were held by Erigena, Roscellinus, William of Occam, Albertus Magnus; and Augustine was finally followed by Aquinas, who is now one of the leading authorities of the Church. Bruno struck out into an altogether different vein of thought.

The reaction against this scientific reading of Genesis naturally came when Christian theology shook off Aristotelianism, and this was brought about indirectly by the opposition to the Arabic science, which also embodied much of Aristotle. Thus the first outspoken opponent of Augustine's teaching, and first champion of literalism, was Suarez, a Jesuit of Spain, a country which had become the second home of Arabic science and philosophy.

No advance whatever in the development of the Evolution idea was made in this long period; scientific speculation and observation were at a standstill except among the Arabs. It is a record of the preservation of the progress towards the idea which the Greeks had made. In the very decades when this progress was stamped out of theology in Spain and Italy, the modern era in the development of the idea was opening in the teachings of Francis Bacon and of the natural philosophers who closely succeeded him.

The Fathers and Schoolmen.

GREGORY OF NYSSA (331-396) taught that Creation was potential. God imparted to matter its fundamental properties and laws. The objects and completed forms of the Universe developed gradually out of chaotic material.

AUGUSTINE (353-430) drew this distinction still more sharply, as Cotterill and Güttler show, between the virtual creation of organisms, the *ratio seminalis*, and the actual visible coming forth of things out of formless matter. All development takes its natural course through the powers imparted to matter by the Creator. Even the corporeal structure of man himself is according to this plan and therefore a product of this natural development. Augustine, as to the origin of life, took his ground half-way between Biogenesis and Abiogenesis. From the beginning there had existed two kinds of germs of living things: first, visible ones, placed by the Creator in animals and plants; and second, invisible ones, latent and becoming active only under certain conditions of combination and temperature. It is these which produce plants and animals in great numbers without any co-operation of existing organisms. Augustine thus sought a naturalistic interpretation of the Mosaic record, or potential rather than special creation, and taught that in the institution of Nature we should not look for miracles but for the laws of Nature. As Moore says: "Augustine distinctly rejected Special Creation in favour of a doctrine which, without any violence to language, we may call a theory of Evolution."

Cotterill traces the history of Augustine's thought upon Genesis. At first he found almost insuperable difficulties in the literal, as contrasted with the allegorical, interpretation. It seems that the account of Creation was a favourite subject of ridicule with the Manichæans, who denied the inspiration of the Old Testament. Thus the outcome of Augustine's studies was a volume entitled *De Genesi contra Manichæos.*

Augustine took a sound philosophical position upon natural causation, and after considering the question of time, and saying that we ought not to think of the six days of the Creation as being equivalent to these solar days of ours, nor of the working of God itself as God now works anything in time, but rather as He has worked from Whom time itself had its beginning. In explaining the passage, "In the beginning God created the heaven and the earth," he says:—

"In the beginning God made the heaven and the earth, as if this were the *seed* of the heaven and the earth, although as yet all the matter of heaven and of earth was in confusion; but because it was certain that from this the heaven and the earth would be, therefore the material itself is called by that name." Again, as in the foregoing passage, in a later passage he speaks of Creation as of things being brought into due order, — "not by intervals of time, but by series of causes, so that those things which in the mind of God were made simultaneously might be brought to their completion by the sixfold representation of that one day."

Of these passages Cotterill remarks:—

"We observe that both the language itself and, yet more, Augustine's profound sense of the impossibility of representing in the forms of finite thought the operations of the infinite and eternal Mind compelled this great theologian to look beyond the mere letter of the inspired history of Creation, and to indicate principles of interpretation which supply by anticipation very valuable guidance, when we compare other conclusions of modern science with this teaching of Holy Scripture."

Cotterill continues that Augustine again illustrates the work of Creation by the growth of a tree from its seed, in which are originally all its various branches and other parts, which do not suddenly spring up such and so large as they are when complete, but in that order with which we are familiar in Nature. All these things are in the seed, not by material substance, but by *causal energy and potency*, and "even so as in the grain itself there were invisible all things simultaneously which were in time to grow into the tree, so the world itself is to be thought of, when God simultaneously created all things, as having at the same time in itself all things that were made in it and with it, when the day itself was created: not only the heaven with the sun and moon and stars, and so forth, but also those things which the water and the earth produced *potentialiter atque causaliter*; before that, in due time, and after long delays, they grew up in such manner as they are now known to us in those works of God which He is working even to the present hour."

With Augustine the progress of comment upon the interpretation of Genesis came nearly to an end. As Güttler observes, men in the cloisters and other centres of culture turned to medicine and ethics; yet, even in this dark period, an occasional friend of the gradual-creation idea appeared. Such was John Scotus Erigena (800–   ), who simply borrowed from Aristotle and Augustine: "From the Uncreated Creating Principles go forth created and self-created beings under the embracing *causæ primordiales*. These *causæ* are equivalent to the Greek 'ideas,' that is the kinds, the eternal forms and unchangeable grounds of reason upon which the world is regulated. Under the influence of the third person of the Godhead, the potentialities of matter are developed, out of which creatures take their origin. In a retrogressive circle, all things return to God"; here Erigena turned to Plato's conception of Final Cause.

THOMAS AQUINAS.—Of much greater influence is the teaching of Thomas Aquinas (1225-1274) as late as the middle of the thirteenth century, for he was and is one of the highest authorities in the Church. He does not contribute to the Evolution idea, but simply expounds Augustine: "As to production of plants, Augustine holds a different view, . . . for some say that on the third day plants were actually produced, each in his kind—a view favoured by the superficial reading of Scripture. But Augustine says that the earth is then said to have brought forth grass and trees *causaliter;* that is, it then received power to produce them." (Quoting Genesis II. 4): "For in those first days, . . . God made creation primarily or *causaliter*, and then rested from His work."

ARABIC SCIENCE AND PHILOSOPHY.

If we now look back several centuries before Aquinas to the Arabs, we find that, while science declined in Europe, it was kept alive, or rather revived, in Arabia. The natural philosophy of the Arabs, which was largely derived from Aristotle, was destined to exert a considerable influence in Europe. Between 813 and 833 Aristotle was translated into Arabic, and his works were soon held in the greatest reverence. Avicenna (980-1037) marked the highest point which science reached in Arabia, and the culmination of the encyclopædic and original studies. Thereafter there was a decline in the East, and about the same period there came the inauguration of scientific and philosophical studies in the West. Between 961 and 976 scientific works were rapidly imported into Spain, and the interest in these subjects became intense.

The three writers from whom we may quote fragments are Avicenna in Arabia, and Avempace and Abubacer in Spain. Draper quotes from Avicenna on the origin of mountains, showing that he was a uniformitarian: —

"Mountains may be due to two causes. Either they are effects of upheavals of the crust of the earth, such as might occur during a violent earthquake, or they are the effect of water, which, cutting for itself a new route, has denuded the valleys, the strata being of different kinds, some soft, some hard. The winds and waters disintegrate the one, but leave the other intact. Most of the eminences of the earth have had this latter origin. It would require a long period of time for all such changes to be accomplished, during which the mountains themselves might be somewhat diminished in size. But that water has been the main cause of these effects, is proved by the existence of fossil remains of aquatic and other animals on many mountains."

This indicates that a careful search through Arabic natural philosophy would probably yield other evidences of knowledge, not only of the uniformity of past and present geological changes, but of the gradual development of life. It is unlikely that the Arabs read Aristotle without extending his theory of the origin of life to their wide survey of Nature.

We take from Güttler the following passages regarding the Spanish philosophers:—

"The Arabic philosophers in Spain threw into a stronger light the natural connection between the inorganic and the organic world. In Avempace's (Ibn-Badja) treatise there are said to exist between men, animals, plants, and minerals, strong relations which bind them into a single and united whole. Through various grades of development, the human soul rises from the level of the instincts which it shares with animals to the 'acquired intellect,' wherein it frees itself more and more from the material and the potential. The 'acquired intellect' is only an elimination of the 'active intellect,' or the Godhead, and thereby it is possible to identify in the last stage of recognition the subject with the object, the thought with the existence."

Avempace, as he was known in Europe, died in 1138. He was succeeded by Abubacer (Ibn-Tophail), who died in 1185.

Abubacer was also a poet, and he handled an analogous theme in an Oriental romance upon the birth of the 'Nature-man':—

"There happens to be under the equator an island, where Man comes into the world without father or mother; by spontaneous generation he arises, directly in the form of a boy, from the earth, while the spirit, which, like the sunshine, emanated from God, unites with the body, growing out of a soft, unformed mass. Without any intelligent surroundings, and without education, this 'Nature-man,' through simple observation of the outer world, and through the combination of various appearances, rises to the knowledge of the world and of the Godhead. First he perceives the individuals, and then he recognizes the various species as independent forms; but as he compares the varieties and species with each other, he comes to the conclusion that they are all sprung from a single animal spirit, and at the same time that the entire animal race forms a single whole. He makes the same discovery among the plants, and finally he sees the animal and plant forms in their unity, and discovers that among all their differences they have sensitiveness and feeling in common; from which he concludes that animals and plants are only one and the same thing."

In the middle of the twelfth century, the translation of the works of the Arabs into Latin began. The Church Provincial Council of Paris in 1209 forbade the study of these Arabic writers, and included Aristotle's *Natural Philosophy* in the interdict, although Albertus Magnus and Thomas Aquinas endeavoured to uphold the orthodoxy of Aristotle against the prejudices which the heretical glosses of Arabic writers had raised against him.

Bruno and Suarez.

In the same year with Bruno, the most extreme rationalist among the theologians in science, was born Suarez, the most extreme conservative.

GIORDANO BRUNO (1548–1600), in his biology, imbibed the diverse influences of the Greeks, of Lucretius, of Arabic philosophy, and of Oriental mysticism, and evolved a highly speculative and vague system of natural philosophy. From the physics of the Stoics he derived the idea that all living beings had a greater or less share of the

Universal Force, a force which leads to steps corresponding in the world of organized beings to a gradated scale of development (like the scale of Aristotle, or, later, of Bonnet, in which each form was a starting-point for the next). Therefore Bruno saw in plants the latent forces of the generation of animals; in stones, the collective kinds of plants; in man, the whole lower creation. Güttler traces Bruno's philosophy to Nicolas of Cusa, and characterizes it as monistic. Lange and Erdmann more accurately speak of his system as pantheistic. In profession, but not in method, Bruno was scientific. He followed Aristotle, and forestalled Bacon, in teaching Induction; one of his chief maxims being that "the investigation of Nature in the unbiased light of reason is our only guide to truth." Bruno's admirers have recently claimed for him anticipation not only of the method of Bacon, but of the 'perfection' doctrine and the theory of monads of Leibnitz, and point out in his physical teachings the theory of the centre of gravity of planets, of the elliptical orbits of comets, and the perfect sphericity of the earth.

By selecting certain passages from his profuse writings, we may credit Bruno with teaching some elements of the Evolution idea; but we must first see how such special passages are enlarged by others, in order to reach Bruno's real conceptions. In estimating his originality, we must be familiar with Greek, Arabic, and Oriental writings, from which he drew as an omnivorous reader. Some of the passages quoted by Brinton and others give a very misleading idea of the real extent of Bruno's grasp, for we unconsciously read into them our present knowledge, as where he says: "The mind of man differs from that of lower animals and of plants, not in quality but in quantity. . . . Each individual is the resultant of innumerable individuals. . . . Each species is the starting-point for the next. . . . No individual is the same to-day as yesterday."

Bruno, with Aristotle, finds that this eternal change is not purposeless, but is ever towards the elimination of defects; hence his alleged anticipation of the optimism of Leibnitz and of the theory of the perfectibility of man. As to 'matter' and 'form,' we again find him following Aristotle in some passages; with him, *Form* seems to stand for the ultimate law of the objective Universe, yet matter is not complete in its forms, because "Nature produces its objects not by subtraction and addition, but only by separation and unfolding. Thus taught the wisest men among the Greeks; and Moses, in describing the origin of life, introduces the universal efficient Being thus speaking: 'Let the earth bring forth the living creature; let the waters bring forth the living creature that hath life'—as though he said—'let matter bring them forth.'" But we find an important departure from Aristotle, where Bruno conceives of matter not as potential but as actual and active.

There is thus great room for difference of opinion as to how far Bruno was an evolutionist in our sense, and we find different authors taking different standpoints according to their greater or less appreciation of the essential elements of the Evolution idea. Lasson holds that Bruno was a follower of Empedocles, and therein a prophet of Darwinism, in the capacity of perfection and the unity of development of organic life. Krause, in his biography of Erasmus Darwin, maintains that Bruno held merely to the identity of the human and animal soul, without actually conceiving their unity of origin. Here enters Aristotelianism again in Bruno's thought, for while he conceived all Evolution as based on endless changes in matter, he describes this movement simply as the outward expression of an indwelling soul. This intelligence is displayed in three grades, which correspond with the steps in the scale of development, because we are free to suppose that "to the sound of the harp of the Universal Apollo (the World Spirit), the lower organisms are called by stages to higher, and the lower stages are connected by intermediate forms with the higher. . . . Every species is first shown in Nature before it passes into life, thus each becomes the starting-point for the next; as in the expansion of the form of the embryo there is an unbroken continuity into the species of man or beast." At other points he speaks as if this soul or intelligence was conceived in a dualistic sense, for he says: "The perfecting power of intelligence does not rest upon another or upon more, but upon the whole."

In Geology, Bruno appears as a uniformitarian, and describes the gradual changes in Nature, not as cataclysmal, but as following their natural course. Thus, he argues against the short six thousand years of the Biblical chronology. This was also not original with Bruno; for he was preceded in the tenth century by Arabic geologists, as seen in the quotation from Avicenna. It is highly probable that Bruno drew upon the Arabs for many other of his scientific ideas.

Finally we may quote a passage from Bruno's satire,—the *Cabala of the Pegasan Horse*, published in 1585, a dialogue between Sabasto and Onorio, in which Bruno affirms the Oriental doctrine of Metempsychosis, and explains his views of the development of organic life. He first compares the animal and human intellect and contrasts monkeys with men in their absence of tool-bearing hands. Speaking of the tongue of the parrot as fitted to utter any sort of sound, he says that the parrot lacks perception and memory equal and akin to man's; then he touches upon the instincts of the parrot and opposes the idea that they are altogether different from the intelligence of man. Then he passes on to say that the lower animals are directed by an unerring intelligence, yet this is not identical with the efficient universal intelligence which directs and causes all to understand. Thus, "above all animals there is an active sense; that is, one which causes all different sensations, and by which all are actually sensitive; and one active intellect, the one, that is, which causes all different understanding and by which all are actively intelligent." He goes on to say that out of the same corporeal material, all bodies are made, and then occurs the following paragraph: "I add this — 'that through diverse causes, habits, orders, measures, and numbers of body and spirit, there are diverse temperaments and natures, different organs are produced, and different genera of things appear.'"

FRANCISCO SUAREZ (1548–1617) was almost the last eminent representative of Scholasticism. Mivart, in his *Genesis of Species*, places him among the post-mediæval theologians of high authority, who devoted a separate section of their works "in opposition to those who maintain the distinct creation of the various kinds — or substantial forms — of organic life." We thus derive the impression that Suarez should be classed with Augustine and Aquinas as a teacher of development; but Huxley in his brilliant article, "Mr. Darwin's Critics,"[1] completely dismisses this enrolment with the Evolutionists, and sets him up as a rigid Special Creationist. He was, in fact, the third great theologian to treat of Creation, and yet as he differed radically in his interpretation of Genesis from both Augustine and Aquinas, he may be

[1] *The Contemporary Review*, 1871.

considered one of the founders of the Special-Creation view as orthodox teaching upon the origin of species, — the teaching which more than any other has led to the schism among the philosophers of Nature. Mivart quotes a number of passages showing that Suarez gave this matter considerable thought. As was later done by Linnæus, Suarez pointed out that there might be some new or post-creation species which were generated by the commingling of original species; he considered the mule and the leopard as instances of this kind.

Huxley also shows that Suarez devotes a special treatise, *Tractatus de opere sex Dierum*, to the discussion of all the problems which arise out of the Mosaic account of Creation; he here reviews the opinions of Philo and Augustine upon these questions, and distinctly rejects them. He suggests that the failure of Aquinas to controvert Augustine's interpretation, arose from his deference to the authority of Augustine, and he maintains that the 'day' of Scripture was a natural day of twenty-four hours, not a period of time as Augustine considered it; he further declares that the entire work of Creation took place in the space of six days. Huxley concludes: —

"As regards the creation of animals and plants, therefore, it is clear that Suarez, so far from distinctly asserting derivative creation, denies it as distinctly and positively as he can; that he is at much pains to refute St. Augustine's opinions; that he does not hesitate to regard the faint acquiescence of St. Thomas Aquinas in the views of his brother-saint, as a kindly subterfuge on the account of Divus Thomas, and that he affirms his own view to be that which is supported by the authority of the Fathers of the Church."

Mivart, in his *Lessons from Nature*, has replied to Huxley, claiming that while Suarez rejected Augustine's view as to the fact of Creation, he testifies as to the validity of the *principles* on which the doctrine of derivative Creation reposes.[1] Yet he is not able to controvert Huxley's exposition of Suarez' real opinions; he does controvert Huxley's statement that Suarez is a leading authority, and quotes Cardinal Norris and others upon the views of Augustine, Albertus Magnus, and Thomas Aquinas, to the effect that these· teachers are still the standards upon these questions.

The truth is that all classes of theologians departed from the original philosophical and scientific standards of some of the Fathers of the Church, and that Special Creation became the universal teaching from the middle of the sixteenth to the middle of the nineteenth centuries. It is the recent establishment of Evolution which has led to the revival of Augustine's broad and true interpretation, and there is no doubt that Mivart's contention so far as the older writers are concerned is correct.

[1] *Lessons from Nature.* London, 1876. Page 447.

The Awakening of Science.

Before speaking of the philosophers who now became the custodians of the Evolution idea and of the speculative writers of the sixteenth and seventeenth centuries, let us glance for a moment at the general advance of knowledge.

Universities in Europe were founded at the beginning of the twelfth century, following those established by the Arabs; Oxford was founded at the beginning of the thirteenth century. During a long period all naturalists were simply compilers. Among these compilers were Clusius, Rondelet, Belon; finally we find Conrad Gesner (1516-1565) writing a complete bibliography of Zoölogy, and leading the naturalists of the sixteenth century. About this time Césalpin (1519-1603) wrote of Vegetable Anatomy, and there sprang up in Padua the School of Anatomy of Vesalius (1514-1564), Fallopius, and his pupil Fabricius, who in turn taught the immortal Harvey. In 1619 Harvey discovered the circulation of the blood and founded Embryology. The systematic classification of animals and plants then arose as a distinct branch in the writings of Ray (1628-1704), Tournefort, and Magnol. Ray was the precursor of Linnæus. In the second half of the seventeenth century and beginning of the eighteenth, the study of the smaller organisms began with Leeuwenhoek, Malpighi, and Swammerdam. "We owe to this period," says St. Hilaire, "the foundation of Microscopy; Anatomy enriched and joined to Physiology; Comparative Anatomy studied with care; Classification placed on a rational and systematic basis." It was these sciences and especially the rise of clearer ideas on the nature of species, which first gave speculation upon Evolution its modern trend, bringing up the origin and the mutability of species as two great central questions.

During these two progressive centuries there were three classes of writers who contributed more or less directly to the foundations of modern Evolution, before its open exposition by Buffon. First, the NATURALISTS, among whom few speculative questions were in vogue, were nevertheless really building up the future materials of thought. Second, the SPECULATIVE EVOLUTIONISTS, who gave a free rein to thoroughly unsound ideas upon the origin of species and preserved many of the early Greek notions. Finally, there were the great NATURAL PHILOSOPHERS, such as Bacon, Descartes, Leibnitz, Hume, ending with the later German school, Kant, Lessing, Herder, and Schelling.

It is a very striking fact, that the basis of our modern methods of studying the Evolution problem was established not by the early naturalists nor by the speculative writers, but by the Philosophers. They alone were upon the main track of modern thought. It is evident that they were groping in the dark for a working theory of the

Evolution of life, and it is remarkable that they clearly perceived from the outset that the point to which observation should be directed was not the past but the present mutability of species, and further, that this mutability was simply the variation of individuals on an extended scale. Thus Variation was brought into prominence as the point to which observation should be directed.

This is one of the contributions of the Philosophers to the history of the Evolution theory. It seems to have sprung up afresh out of the advances in Biology of the previous century, for it was something which is not found among the Greeks. It was Bacon who pointed out the evidence for Variation in animals and plants, and the bearing of this upon the production of new species and upon the gradations of life. Leibnitz took a second step in indicating that the Evolution of life was a necessary part of a system of cosmic philosophy, and although wholly at sea in his theory of Evolution, he added to the evidence for it by giving examples of gradations of character between living and extinct forms, as proofs of the universal gradation or connection between species. Thus, among these philosophers we find pointed out the gradations of type, the facts of variation, and the bearing of these facts upon the production of new species, also the analogy between artificial selection practised by man in producing new forms and the production of new forms in Nature.

These were original departures, in which these writers were thoroughly logical and sound, and were laying foundations for those observations which finally led to the establishment of the Evolution theory. Yet it must not be inferred that the Evolution of life was a very prominent element in their philosophy.

In the larger aspect of their teaching, namely, in the broad question of Evolution itself as the law of the Universe, they all found their inspiration in Greek literature. Bacon did not put forth a general Evolution system; Descartes and Leibnitz, who were the first to do so, drew from Greek poetry and philosophy, and the same is true of all the later philosophers. Kant and the later German philosophers drew not only from these sources, but from suggestions found in contemporary science, from Linnæus and especially from Buffon. It is very probable also that careful search among the earlier naturalists would reveal an anticipation of some of the problems which are set forth in Bacon and Leibnitz.

Their first great gift, as we have said, was in establishing the right trend to observation; their second gift was the outcome of their battle for the principle of natural causation. From Bacon to Kant, who, it is true, wavered in advocating this principle, this was a theme of the first rank; that is, the operation of natural causes in the world rather than of the constant interference of a Creator in his works. In the doubts which were felt as to natural causation, we see proofs of the close relations between the Church, the State, and Science, and that this principle, as well as that of Evolution, was under the ban of unorthodoxy.

THE NATURAL PHILOSOPHERS.

FRANCIS BACON (1561-1626) thought lightly of Greek science. He strongly condemned the reverence for it as a bar to progress, and in his sweeping criticisms was far too severe, especially upon Aristotle, in whom he undoubtedly found his famous principles of induction.

> "Nor," he says, "must we omit the opinion or, rather, prophecy of an Egyptian priest in regard to the Greeks, that they would forever remain children without any antiquity of knowledge, or knowledge of antiquity; for they certainly have this in common with children, that they are prone to talking and incapable of generation, their wisdom being loquacious and unproductive of effects. Hence the external signs derived from the origin and birthplace of our philosophy are not favourable."

He failed to appreciate Greek suggestiveness, and little foresaw the influence it was destined to exert in framing modern Evolution. If we are to judge Bacon himself by his maxims and aphorisms, no place would be too high for him; but judging him by his actual researches and practices, and carefully estimating his real influence upon posterity, we must place him below Harvey, whose brilliant application of the inductive method in science he is said to have ignored.

In the *Advancement of Learning* (Book V.) he points out the art of indication. "For indication proceeds (1) from experiment to experiment, or (2) from experiment to axioms, which may again point out new experiments. The former we call learned experience, and the latter the interpretation of Nature, Novum Organum, or new machine of mind." This 'art' substantially implies the use of the working hypothesis. That Bacon, as early as 1620, fully grasped the wealth of knowledge, which could be gained from observation, experiment, and induction, is shown repeatedly in the course of his works. The following passages are cited because they bear especially upon the question of species, and show that Bacon was one of the first, if not the first, to raise the problem of the *mutability of species* as possibly a result of the accumulation of *variations*. He speaks, in the first place, of variations of an extreme kind (*Novum Organum*, Book II., Section 29).

"In the eighth rank of prerogative instances, we will place deviating instances, such as the errors of Nature or strange and monstrous objects, in which Nature deviates and turns from her ordinary course. For the errors of Nature differ from singular instances, inasmuch as the latter are the miracles of species, the former of the individuals. Their use is much the same, for they rectify the understanding in opposition to habit, and reveal common forms. For with regard to these, also, we must not desist from inquiry till we discern the cause of the deviation; the cause does not, however, in such cases rise to a regular form, but only in the latent process towards such a form, for he who is acquainted with the paths of Nature will more readily observe their deviations, and *vice versâ*, he who has learnt her deviations will be able more accurately to describe her paths."

Having thus spoken of deviations or variations, and of the necessity of understanding the normal type in order to detect the variation, also of the desirability of studying the cause of the variation, Bacon proceeds to point out that it is possible for man to produce variations experimentally, and shows that living objects are well adapted to experimental work:—

"They differ again from singular instances, by being much more apt for practice and the operative branch. For it would be very difficult to generate new species, but less so to vary known species, and thus produce many rare and unusual results. The passage from the miracles of Nature to those of Art is easy; for if Nature be once seized in her variations and the cause be manifest, it will be easy to lead her by Art to such variation as she was first led to by chance; and not only to that, but others, since deviations on the one side lead and open the way to others in every direction."

In the above passage Bacon points out that in artificial selection we take advantage of the chance variations of Nature, and accumulate them. In the next passage he points out the presence of transitional forms in Nature between two types (Section 30.):

"In the ninth rank of prerogative instances we will place bordering instances, which we are also wont to term participants. They are such as exhibit those species of bodies which appear to be composed of two species, or to be the rudiments between one and the other. They may well be classed with the singular or heteroclite instances; for in the whole system of things, they are rare and extraordinary. Yet from their dignity they must be treated of and classed separately, for they point out admirably the order and constitution of things, and suggest the causes of the number and quality of the more common species in the Universe, leading the understanding from that which is, to that which is possible. We have examples of them in Moss, which is something between putrescence and a plant; in some Comets, which hold a place between stars and ignited meteors; in Flying Fishes, between fishes and birds; and in Bats, between birds and quadrupeds."

Bacon also observed " that plants sometimes degenerate to the point of changing into other plants," but so far as I know gave no grounds of support for this opinion. These quotations show that even at the beginning of the seventeenth century, the mutability of species was a live question, which was being more or less discussed, and that mutability was seen in its modern bearings upon Evolution.

Bacon went further, and in his *Nova Atlantis* we find he projects the establishment of a Scientific Institution, to be devoted to the progress of the natural sciences, for experiments upon the metamorphoses of organs and observations upon what causes species to vary; for researches which would reveal the manner in which species had multiplied and become diversified in a state of Nature. After three centuries this project is materializing so that one of our new experimental stations might well be called the Baconian Institute of Experimental Evolution.

The central idea of the grand Evolution of life is frequently implied rather than clearly expressed in Bacon's writings. He differed from Descartes and later philosophers in proposing the method by which the natural system of the Universe could be ascertained, rather than in speculating upon the system itself.

RENE DESCARTES (1596–1650) threw off the yoke of Scholasticism in France as Bacon had in England. His thought took an entirely different turn, rather the philosophical than the scientific. In his *Principes de la Philosophie*, published in 1637, he cautiously advanced his belief that the physical universe is a mechanism, and that as such it is explicable upon physical principles. Buffon credits him with taking here the most daring step possible in philosophy, in attempting to explain all things upon principles of natural law. There is no doubt that at the time Descartes took this step, it required even greater moral courage than his, to break away from the prevailing dogmas as to Special Creation. In a passage upon Creation, which Huxley aptly terms a singular exhibition of force and weakness, Descartes wavers between his conviction as to the true order of things, and the prevailing teaching:

He marks the difference between the natural order of gradual development and the unnatural doctrine of sudden creation, which at the time had become the prevailing and prescribed teaching. Further, he intimates that all things are ordered by natural laws:

"All the same, if we can imagine a few intelligible and simple principles upon which the stars, and earth, and all the visible world might have been produced (although we well know that it has not been produced in this fashion), we reach a better understanding of the nature of all things than if we describe simply how things now are, or how we believe them to have been, created. Because I believe I have discovered such principles, I shall endeavour to explain them."

GOTTFRIED WILHELM LEIBNITZ (1646–1716), the first of the great philosophers of Germany, advocated two ideas in his writings which exerted a great and widely misleading influence in Biology. The first was his doctrine of Continuity, and the second, his doctrine of Perfectibility in the Monads. The law of Perfectibility is said to have been suggested by Bruno, but as applied to the animal creation certainly came more or less directly from Aristotle. It is surprising to find how Leibnitz' principle of Continuity adapted itself to the idea of Evolution of organic beings. In part from observations of his own, and probably in part influenced by Aristotle, Leibnitz expressed the law of Continuity as applied to life as follows: "All natural orders of beings present but a single chain, in which the different classes of animals, like so many rings, are so closely united that it is not possible either by observation or imagination to determine where one ends or begins."

He was very familiar both with Bacon and Descartes, and by the former had probably had his attention called to the matter of Variation.

Leibnitz' main teachings, as in part a revival of Aristotle's, certainly had an entirely different trend from those of Bacon and Descartes. He stimulated the speculations of Diderôt, Maupertuis, Bonnet, Robinet, and others, of the speculative writers; in short, he founded a 'school' with his Continuity doctrines. On the other hand, like Bacon, he appears, in such passages as those quoted above, to have especially directed research to those natural gradations between species which have become the pillars of Evolution.

SPINOZA (1632–1677) took a similar but firmer ground in regard to natural causation: "The natural laws and principles by which all things are made and some forms are changed into others, are everywhere and through all time the same." To PASCAL (1623–1662) was attributed by Geoffroy St. Hilaire a thoroughly evolutionistic view as to the origin of animals and plants; yet diligent search by other authors has failed to locate this in any of his writings. In the close of his treatise upon Optics, NEWTON (1642–1727) pointed out the uniformity of structure which pervades all animal types. HUME (1711–1776) also concluded that the world might have been generated rather than created by the activity of its own inherent principles, and Leslie Stephens points out that he also considered the 'survival of the fittest' principle.

In those days of few printed books and concentrated thought, such scattered suggestions as these generated into opinions and theories. They are the minor features of the environment of the Evolution idea. The final and the fullest expression of Evolution in philosophical literature is found in Kant.

EMMANUEL KANT (1724–1804) was born sixteen years after Buffon and Linnæus, and therefore thought and wrote after natural history had made very great advances. The ideas of Selection, Adaptation, Environment, and Inheritance, which are attributed to him as original by Haeckel, are also found in the works of Buffon. Buffon's most extreme views were expressed between 1760–70, while Kant's extreme views were expressed between 1757 and 1771.

We owe to Schultze a very full exposition of all the passages in the writings of the great Königsberg philosopher which bear upon the Evolution theory. In his earlier years (1755), Kant published a work entitled *The General History of Nature and Theory of the Heavens*, embracing an attempt to reconcile Newton and Leibnitz, or Nature from the mechanical and teleological standpoints. At this time he was attracted by the mechanism of Lucretius. Haeckel points out, that in this work Kant took a very advanced position as to the domain of natural causation, or, as Haeckel terms it, 'mechanism in the domain of life,' while in his later work (1790), his criticism of *The Teleological Faculty of Judgment*, he took a much more conservative position.

In the former, he considers all Nature under the domain of natural causes, while in the latter, he divides Nature into the 'inorganic' in which natural causes prevail, and the 'organic' in which the active teleological principle prevails. There was, therefore, in Kant's later work a cleft between primeval matter and the domain of life; for in the latter he assumed the presence of final causes acting for definite ends. As Haeckel says:—

"After having quite correctly maintained the origin of organic forms out of raw matter by mechanical laws (in the manner of crystallization), as well as a gradual development of the different species by descent from one common original parent, Kant adds, 'but he, the archæologist of Nature, that is the paleontologist, must for this end ascribe to the common mother, an organization ordained purposely with a view to the needs of all her offspring, otherwise the possibility of suitability of form in the products of the animal and vegetable kingdoms cannot be conceived at all.'"

Of course we cannot here follow out all the reasons for Kant's change of view from his earlier to his later years; we simply see that he was staggered by the impossibility of human investigation ever reaching an explanation of the laws which have governed the derivation of all organic beings, from polyps to men; he declared that this doctrine (of Evolution) was compatible with the mechanical conception of Nature, although no natural science can attain it; it would therefore remain a daring flight of reason. In a striking passage upon the limits of our knowledge, he says:—

"It is quite certain that we cannot become sufficiently acquainted with organized creatures and their hidden potentialities by aid of purely mechanical natural principles, much less can we explain them; and this is so certain, that we may boldly assert that it is absurd for man even to conceive such an idea, or to hope that a Newton may one day arise even to make the production of a blade of grass comprehensible, according to natural laws ordained by no intention; such an insight we must absolutely deny to man."

As Haeckel observes, Darwin rose up as Kant's Newton; for he offered an explanation of the production and of the development of those very structures and adaptations in Nature, which remained wholly unexplained until 1858. Haeckel expresses evident disappointment at Kant's position; yet this position may be regarded as raising Kant higher in the scale of science, if not of philosophy. If he could not even conceive of any natural law whereby these beautiful adaptations of Nature could be explained, he was not justified in making a bold assumption of the existence of such a law. The feeling that Newton and other physical philosophers had supplied the inorganic world with its regulating principles would have made it logical for Kant, like Descartes, to carry his reasoning a step further into the world of life. But his logic and philosophy were held back by his scientific instinct for evidence, and evidence was then wholly lacking; for even the explanation offered by Lamarck was not available.

Kant was undoubtedly familiar with the writings

of Buffon and Maupertuis; he alludes to them both; in his second work, prepared in 1757, but not published until much later, it is evident that his standpoint towards Evolution was very similar to that of Buffon in what we call his 'middle period.' Later, in 1763, he parallels Buffon in tracing back all the higher forms of life to simpler elementary forms. He traces the changes produced in man by migration, differences of climate and the like, and deduces the law of degeneration from the originally created types of species. In 1771 he also brings man into the ranks of Nature, and alludes to his former quadrupedal attitude, here agreeing with Buffon and Helvetius. In his study upon the races of man we also find that he expresses the principle of Survival of the Fittest, as applied to groups of organisms, very much in the form in which it had been stated by Buffon. In this connection he quotes Maupertuis. He also sees the force of accidental variation and of artificial selection in the production of certain external colours.

Kant's comprehensive view of Evolution, and his hesitation as to the problem of causation, is all summed up in the following remarkable passage (1790), quoted by Schultze:—

"It is desirable to examine the great domain of organized beings by means of a methodical comparative anatomy, in order to discover whether we may not find in them something resembling a system, and that too in connection with their mode of generation, so that we may not be compelled to stop short with a mere consideration of forms as they are — which gives us no insight into their generation — and need not despair of gaining a full insight into this department of Nature. The agreement of so many kinds of animals in a certain common plan of structure, which seems to be visible not only in their skeletons, but also in the arrangement of the other parts — so that a wonderfully simple typical form, by the shortening and lengthening of some parts, and by the suppression and development of others, might be able to produce an immense variety of species — gives us a ray of hope, though feeble, that here perhaps some results may be obtained, by the application of the principle of the *mechanism of Nature*, without which, in fact, no science can exist. This analogy of forms (in so far as they seem to have been produced in accordance with a common prototype, notwithstanding their great variety) strengthens the supposition that they have an actual blood-relationship, due to derivation from a common parent; a supposition which is arrived at by observation of the graduated approximation of one class of animals to another, beginning with the one in which the principle of purposiveness seems to be most conspicuous, namely man, and extending down to the polyps, and from these even down to mosses and lichens, and arriving finally at raw matter, the lowest stage of Nature observable by us. From this raw matter and its forces, the whole apparatus of Nature seems to have been derived according to mechanical laws (such as those which resulted in the production of crystals); yet this apparatus, as seen in organic beings, is so incomprehensible to us, that we feel ourselves compelled to conceive for it a different principle. But it would seem that the archæologist of Nature is at liberty to regard the great *Family* of creatures (for as a Family we must conceive it, if the above-mentioned continuous and connected relationship has a real foundation) as having sprung from the immediate results of her earliest revolutions, judging from all the laws of their mechanisms known to or conjectured by him."

What a connecting link between all past and future thought lies in this great passage! We can trace the influence of every earlier philosopher from Aristotle down, and recognize the problems which have faced every later one.

LESSING'S (1729-1781) views of Cosmology included the doctrine of a law of development which embraced all Nature, and led him also to the idea of a gradated scale of organisms.

JOHANN GOTTFRIED HERDER (1744-1803) was a student of Kant in Königsberg between 1762 and 1764. We have seen that Kant's earliest contribution to the Evolution theory was published in 1755, so that it is probable that Herder came under the influence of Kant's earlier views. As shown by Bärenbach, who has made a special study of this side of his philosophy in his *Herder als Vorgänger Darwin's*. Herder was less cautious than his master, and appears almost as a literal prophet of the modern natural philosophy. In a general way he upholds the doctrine of the transformation of the lower and higher forms of life, of a continuous transformation from lower to higher types, and of the law of Perfectibility. "Every combination of force and form," he says, "is neither stability nor retrogression, but progress. Take off the outer shell and there is no death in Nature. Every disturbance marks the transfer to a higher type." In his *Ideen zur Geschichte der Menschheit*, published in Tübingen in 1806, we find the following passage:—

"A certain unity of type pervades all the different forms of life, like a main type which can display the widest variations.

Similarities of external and, still more, of internal, structure pervade all the land animals and are repeated in man. The amphibia, birds, fishes, insects, water animals, depart in widening degrees from this main type, which is lost in the plant and inorganic creation. Our vision reaches no further, but all these transfers render it not improbable that in the series of extinct forms the same type, in a ruder and simpler form, may have prevailed. We can, therefore, assume that, according to their nearness to man, all beings have their greater or less likeness to him, and that the nature of all life seems to conform to a main single plasticity of organization."

We see here that Herder clearly formulated the doctrine of *unity of type*, which prevailed among all the evolutionists of the period immediately following.

FRIEDRICH WILHELM JOSEPH SCHELLING (1775-1854) at the age of twenty published his *Ideen zur einer Philosophie der Natur*. Here he first unfolded his ideas of the Philosophy of Nature, Kant having spoken of the science of Nature. One section of his philosophy was followed and developed by Oken, but Schelling was greatly admired also by Kielmeyer, and undoubtedly exercised great influence upon Goethe. Isidore St. Hilaire pays him a high tribute, and speaks at length of the admiration felt for Schelling in France; he places him midway between the general philosopher, typified by the more metaphysical writers, and the philosopher of natural objects, such as Geoffroy St. Hilaire. Schelling independently arrived at the conclusion of Kielmeyer, that all the functions of life are but the diverse modifications of a single force.

We here meet with a natural culmination of the progress of the Evolution idea in philosophy, caused by this departure from induction.

For Schelling's method was deductive, and he sought in deduction the main sources of human knowledge. At the point of empiricism, where, according to Cuvier, science ends, he held that true science begins. By this he meant, that if the human reason can question and answer upon its own existence, and upon its relations to the Creator, it can also answer upon all Creation; it can comprehend and reconstruct the order of the Universe. "To philosophize upon Nature, it is to create Nature." Because the hypothesis springs from the mind, and is merely tested by experiment, he places the direct fruits of hypothesis or deductive science above inductive science. This might be termed a reversion to Greek natural philosophy or methods of thought brilliant but unproductive of fixed results.

IV.

THE EVOLUTIONISTS OF THE EIGHTEENTH CENTURY.

Die Idee der Metamorphose ist eine höchst ehrwürdige, aber zugleich höchst gefährliche Gabe von oben. Die führt ins Formlose, zerstört das Wissen, löst es auf. — GOETHE.

BESIDE the philosophers between Bacon and Kant we distinguish two other classes of evolutionists during the latter part of the seventeenth and the whole of the eighteenth century. These are, first, the speculative writers from Duret to Oken, partly philosophers, partly naturalists and of other professions, who resuscitated some of the crude, as well as some of the valuable scientific hypotheses of the Greeks; and second, the great naturalists of the eighteenth century, who, with the philosophers, laid the real foundations of the modern Evolution idea.

THE SPECULATIVE EVOLUTIONISTS.

The lists of speculative writers are not yet complete. Among the curiosities of Evolution literature are included the works of Duret, the mayor of a town in France, also of Kircher and Bonnami, two priests. Of real interest are the speculations of Maupertuis, a mathematician and astronomer; of Diderôt, the political writer; of Bonnet, the eminent naturalist; of De Maillet, French consul at Leghorn;

of Robinet, one of the popular scientists of his time; and finally of Oken, professor of natural history in the University of Zurich during the first third of the present century. Some surprise may be felt at my placing Oken in this group, for his *Physio-Philosophie*, and his '*Ur-Schleim* Theorie,' are considered by some to raise him high as a prophet of Modern Evolution.

Yet Oken is a fair exponent; in his 'sea-foam' and 'spontaneous generation' vagaries we find him drawing from such an ancient and imaginative authority as Anaximander. In fact, when we analyze his contributions we find that they actually represent the last survivals of Greek Evolution with a veneer of eighteenth-century progress. When we read him through and through we see that he is about as truly an anachronism as old Claude Duret of 1609.

This is more or less true of all these speculators. They were not actually in the main Evolution movement; they were either out of date or upon the side tracks of thought. They can be sharply distinguished from both the naturalists and philosophers in the fact that their speculations advanced without the support of observation, and without the least deference to inductive canons. Several of them were very popular writers, and unchecked speculation was so much their characteristic that they undoubtedly retarded the development of the true Evolution idea by drawing ridicule upon all genuine search for a naturalistic explanation of the phenomena of life.

We find them reviving Greek ideas both in the spontaneous origin of life in different forms and in metamorphoses and transformations, hardly less sudden than those of Empedocles. Another source of their authority is the highly imaginative natural history literature of the Middle Ages. In all this chaff there is of course some wheat, as is often the case in speculation unhindered by observation. Lines of suggestion coming near to modern thought upon heredity are found especially in the essays of Maupertuis, who drew from Democritus and Anaxagoras. De Maillet outlined the theory of 'transmission of acquired characters' in a crude form similar to that of Empedocles. Robinet conceived Evolution on a large scale, borrowing a mistaken interpretation of Aristotle. Oken stated somewhat more distinctly than had been done previously the hypothesis of the cellular origin of life. As Bonnet was the contemporary of Buffon, and Oken lived thirty years later than Lamarck, the study of this group carries us well beyond the period in which the sound foundations of Modern Evolution were laid.

We are indebted to Ducasse and Varigny for pointing out some of the quaint early biological literature of the seventeenth century. CLAUDE DURET in his *Histoire Admirable des Plantes*, published in 1609, is a direct transformationist. Among other remarkable tales he describes and figures a tree, 'not, it is true, common in France, but frequently observed in Scotland' (a country which the Mayor evidently considered so remote that his observation would probably not be gainsaid); from this tree leaves are falling; upon one side they strike the water and slowly transform into fishes, upon the other they strike land and turn into birds. FATHER BONNAMI was another writer of similar comedies. In the latter part of the century appeared the *Mundus Subterraneus* of FATHER KIRCHER (Amsterdam, 1678, 2 vols.); this is full of 'authentic observations' of the same stamp. The worthy priest describes orchids giving birth to birds and even to very small men; this occurs when they touch the ground where a sort of fecundation occurs by the *spermaticus humor superfluus humo sparsus — ubi congressus factus est.*

BENOÎT DE MAILLET (1656-1738) did not pause long over the dry facts within the reach of contemporary natural science in his famous *Telliamed.* In his earlier years, before this book was written, we learn that he was a careful student of Geology and Paleontology, and that he perceived the true nature and origin of fossils. This in itself entitles him to considerable credit, when we remember that at the time there were wide differences of opinion regarding fossils. Natural theology found in them proofs of the universal Deluge, while such an acute thinker as Voltaire, who scoffed alternately at religion and science, claimed that the shells on the mountain-tops had been thrown aside by pilgrims on their journeys to Rome, and that petrified fishes were the remains of their unfinished repasts.

It was probably his readings among the Greeks, as well as his own paleontological and geological studies, which gave De Maillet his central hypothesis that all terrestrial animals had their origin in marine forms by direct descent; that birds were derived from flying fishes, lions from sea-lions, and man from *l'homme marin*, the husband of the mermaid! De Maillet soberly collected all the narratives of the mermaid, which were abundant in the literature of that period, then reasoning that the mermaid must have espoused, derived man from the metamorphosis of her husband.

These extravagant ideas are mingled with the rudiments of a principle. For De Maillet, in every case, endeavours to explain this metamorphosis, or transformation, by the influences of environment and habit. The aquatic organism finds its way upon land; there its new surroundings of air and herbage, and its efforts to accommodate itself, are followed by a series of modifications. In modern terms, 'it acquires new characters.' The rash feature of De Maillet's views is, that he believes these modifications take place within the short period of a single life; they are then transmitted to the descendants, which do not revert to the aquatic form. Thus, in his account of the origin of birds, he describes flying fishes as, "driven out of the water by the ardour of the chase or by pursuit, or carried by the wind, they might have fallen some distance from the shore among plants, which, while supplying them with food, prevented them from returning to the water. Here, under the influence of the air, their anterior fins with their raised membranes transformed into wings, barbules, and feathers, the skin became covered with down, the ventral fins became limbs, the body was remodelled, the neck and the beak became elongated, and the fish discovered itself a bird."

Huxley speaks as if scant justice had been done to Maillet, but we must infer that he has not thoroughly examined the remarkable metamorphoses of which the above is a moderate example. St. Hilaire more critically and justly says:—

"Quant à De Maillet, qui fait naître les oiseaux des poissons volants, les reptiles des poissons rampants, et les hommes des tritons, ses rêveries, en partie renouvelées d'Anaximandre, ont leur place marquée, non dans l'histoire de la science, mais dans celle des aberrations de l'esprit humain."

His remarkable theories were expounded in 1749, and republished in 1756; the letters of the title of his book reversed those of his own name,— *Telliamed, ou Entretiens d'un philosophe indien avec un missionaire français sur la diminution de la Mer.* The argument is sustained in a dialogue which is of a thoroughly reverent character, De Maillet endeavouring to show that his system conforms to the teachings of Genesis. He interpreted the days of Genesis as so many gradual periods or epochs, holding that the first period of life was preceded by a universal Deluge, and that the origin of life began with the gradual recession of the sea from the earth. Here re-enters the favourite Greek doctrine of pre-existing germs. These germs were predetermined as to the forms to which they should give rise, but only those forms developed to which the gradually changing environment was favourable. Thus, the lower forms of life appeared while the waters were still in excess, while, as the waters receded, higher and higher forms arose. But the scene of development was invariably the sea; the germs gave rise to no land forms direct, but land forms were always developed by transformation from marine forms. Thus, all organisms were arranged in two series: first, the aquatic and marine, springing directly from the germs; and second, the terrestrial and aerial, arising by metamorphosis from the marine.

In these transformations De Maillet was not embarrassed by the fixity of characters or by the fact that no such metamorphoses had ever been witnessed. Yet, we find buried in all this fiction two suggestions of theory. De Maillet claims for the scientist the right to search into Nature direct for her secrets. He finds in the world proofs that the days of Genesis were great epochs of time, and he suggests in his metamorphoses, absurd as they are, the idea of the modification of organisms by environment and habit, and the transmission of these modifications to the descendants; in other words, he advocates the 'transmission of acquired characters.'

PETER LOUIS MOREAU DE MAUPERTUIS (1698–1759) was a French mathematician and astronomer of considerable reputation in his day. As one of the most prominent members of the eighteenth-century French circle in Berlin, he was elected President of the Berlin Academy in 1746.

His contributions to the Evolution idea are pointed out by Perrier. We see in them the influence of Leibnitz, and learn that the reputation of Maupertuis suffered from his having borrowed other ideas of the German philosopher in a paper which he advanced upon the Conservation of Energy doctrine. In an obscure article, *Système de la Nature: Essai sur la Formation des Corps Organises* (1751), which has been unearthed in the course of the present diligent search for all the prophecies of Evolution, we find that Maupertuis had an original theory as to the nature of living matter; that he advanced an hypothesis of generation very similar to that of Darwin, and also a theory of the origin of new species. He did not anticipate the 'Evolution' or *emboîtement* of Bonnet, but advanced an hypothesis of transformism, based upon the idea that all material particles are in some degree invested with the psychical properties of the higher organisms; in other words, the monistic idea. By this assumption of the investment of non-living matter with the properties of living matter, he was in a position to readily derive the latter from the former, and to directly unite the animate and inanimate worlds. He does not enter into detail as to the origin of life, but carries us a step further in his ideas of heredity, somewhat on the lines of Democritus, and of Buffon, who had published his similar 'theory of generation' five years earlier (1746).

"The elementary particles which form the embryo are each drawn from the corresponding structure in the parent, and conserve a sort of recollection (*souvenir*) of their previous form, so that in the offspring they will reflect and reproduce a resemblance to the parents. . . . If some of the particles happen to be missing, an imperfect being is formed . . . if the elements of the different species are united, a hybrid is produced. . . . In some cases a child resembles one of his ancestors more than even its parents; in this case we may suppose that the material particles conserve more strongly the habits they possessed in the ancestral form."

Maupertuis thus gives us a theory which resembles both the 'Pangenesis' of Darwin and the 'Perigenesis' of Haeckel.[1]

These principles of reproduction and heredity enable Maupertuis to explain readily the origin of new species, and here again we find a striking anticipation of one modern doctrine of the cause of

---

[1] In Haeckel's "Perigenesis of the plastidules," we have a theory of heredity based upon the assumption that the material hereditary particles preserve a power of repetition of former states analogous to that witnessed in memory.

fortuitous variation: We can, he says, thus readily explain how new species are formed, . . . by supposing that the elementary particles may not always retain the order which they present in the parents, but may fortuitously produce differences, which, multiplying and accumulating, have resulted in the infinite variety of species which we see at the present time. The modifications arising from different habits cause the varieties thus formed to be sterile *inter se;* thus these new species are kept separate.

Evolution, according to this hypothesis, advances by fortuity, by the chance combinations of hereditary elements which produce new characters. Divergence is continued and fostered by physiological isolation.

DENIS DIDERÔT[1] (1713-1784) must also be ranked as one of the speculative contributors to the theory of the origin of species. Perrier points out that it was an essay published in 1751 by Maupertuis, under an assumed name, which called forth Diderôt's *Pensées sur L'Interprétation de la Nature*, published in 1754. He leaves aside the question of the nature of inorganic material particles, and begins his system by endowing all organic particles with a sort of rudimentary sensibility, which

[1] Denis Diderôt, the famous man of letters of the middle of the eighteenth century, became an opponent of the teleological teaching of the day. He is believed to have contributed to D'Holbach's *Système de la Nature*, which was characterised as the Bible of Atheism. The passages quoted, however, indicate that Diderôt was a theist.

impels them to constantly change their position in search for the most favourable position,—a form of the attraction and repulsion doctrine of Empedocles applied to organic particles: "The animal," he says, "is a system of different organic molecules, which, impelled by dim sensations similar to those of obtuse and vague touch,—sensations which have been imparted to them by Him who created matter in general,—have combined, until each has found the position most suitable to its form and to its repose. This position may be changed by the innumerable disturbances caused by an access of new particles which have not yet obtained their repose."

He proceeds by asking the question, whether plants and animals have always been what they now are, then continuing in a spirit similar to that of Descartes, he revives the Anaxagorean doctrine of pre-existent germs in a modified form:—

"Even if Revelation teaches us that species left the hands of the Creator as they now are, the philosopher who gives himself up to conjecture comes to the conclusion that life has always had its elements scattered in the mass of inorganic matter; that it finally came about that these elements united; that the embryo formed of this union has passed through an infinitude of organization and development; that it has acquired, in succession, movement, sensation, ideas, thought, reflection, conscience, emotions, signs, gestures, articulation, language, laws, and finally the sciences and arts; that millions of years have elapsed during each of these phases of development, and that there are still new developments to be taken which are as yet unknown to us."

The hypothesis of Diderôt does not imply his advocacy of an 'internal perfecting tendency,' for his particles do not arrange themselves in any predetermined order. It is rather a form of the Survival of the Fittest theory applied, not to entire organisms, but to the particles of which it is composed. Blind and ceaseless trials, such as those imagined by Empedocles, Democritus, and Lucretius, are made by these particles, impelled by their rude sensibility. As a sequel of many failures, finally a favourable combination is formed, which persists until a recombination is rendered necessary.

I have met another passage by Diderôt, quoted in Morley's biography (II. p. 91), which Morley (not knowing of Empedocles' hypothesis) speaks of as an anticipation of a famous modern theory, referring of course to 'Natural Selection.' This is especially valuable because it affords another conclusive proof that the idea of the 'Survival of the Fittest' must actually be traced back to Empedocles, six centuries before Christ. It is contained in an imaginary dialogue upon the teleological view of Nature between 'Saunderson' and the 'Professor':—

"I may at least ask of you, for example, who told you — you and Leibnitz and Clarke and Newton — that in the first instances of the formation of animals, some were not without heads and others without feet? I may mention . . . that all the faulty combinations of matter disappeared, and that those individuals only survived whose mechanism implied no important misadaptation (contradiction), and who had the power of supporting and perpetuating themselves."

CHARLES BONNET (1720-1793) was in no modern sense an evolutionist, although he was long known as such and was the author of the term. He derived it from *e-volvo* to express his remarkable theory of life, which was an adaptation of Leibnitz' philosophy to embryology. The term became a *nomen nudum* when the doctrine of 'Epigenesis' replaced that of 'Evolution,' and was finally taken up by, and applied as appropriate to, our modern doctrine of development. We recall, in passing, the great and prolonged discussions during the eighteenth and the early part of the nineteenth century, between the 'evolutionist' and 'epigenetic' school of embryonic development, as absorbing an immense amount of time and energy and diverting the attention of naturalists from the greater problem of the genesis of species.

When we examine Bonnet's 'Evolution or expansion of the invisible into visibility' and absence of generation in the strict sense of the term, we find it difficult to believe that Cuvier, and many other eminent naturalists, were among Bonnet's supporters. Erasmus Darwin was among his opponents, and we see in his *Zoonomia* a quaint criticism of Bonnet's extravagant hypothesis:—

"Many ingenious philosophers have found so great difficulty in conceiving the manner of reproduction in animals, that they have supposed all the numerous progeny to have existed in miniature in the animal originally created. This idea, besides its being unsupported by any analogy we are acquainted with, ascribes a greater continuity to organized matter than we can readily admit, . . .

these embryons . . . must possess a greater degree of minuteness than that which was ascribed to the devils who tempted St. Anthony, of whom twenty thousand were said to have been able to dance a saraband on the point of a needle without the least incommoding each other."

We become more charitable in judging Bonnet as a man of science when we learn that, beginning in 1740, while associated with Réaumur in the University of Geneva, he made a series of admirable observations and original discoveries, such as those upon 'parthenogenesis' in the Aphides or Tree Lice, the mode of reproduction in the Bryozoa, the respiration of insects, and that it was the unfortunate failure of his eyesight in 1754 which turned him from observation to speculation. His speculations were as unsound as his observations had been sound and valuable.

Bonnet, in 1764, published his *Contemplations de la Nature*, and in 1768 his *Palingénésie Philosophique, ou idées sur l'état passé et sur l'état des Êtres vivants*. The latter work is dedicated "to the friends of Truth and of Virtue, who are mine."

Bonnet found his inspiration in the law of Continuity of Leibnitz, and along different lines of reasoning he reached the same conclusion as the great German philosopher, that no such thing as generation, in the strict sense of the term, occurs in Nature. Leibnitz' law of Continuity he expands into the idea that all creation forms a continuous chain from the mineral up to the top of the animal world. In the present order of life there are no successive acts of creation, as is generally believed by those who attempt to adapt the discoveries of Palæontology to the Mosaic account. The Universe moves on by its own internal forces, and the whole of organic life was contained preformed in the germs of the first beings. Life thus forms a scale of absolutely unbroken individuals; the varieties form links from species to species; the first term of this chain is the atom, the last is the most elevated of cherubim; the chain is not broken by death, for the individual is the bearer of all future germs. Here we find an adumbration of the 'immortality or continuity of the germ-plasm' in relation to the death of the individual.

Added to this law of Continuity, is an Aristotelian 'internal perfecting principle,' which causes these germs to pass from the mineral to the plant, from the plant to the animal, from the animal to man. In these transformations, Bonnet does not seem to have been deterred by his anatomical knowledge, nor to have in the least degree embodied the ideas of transformism which were then being advanced by Buffon; he believes that the appearance of higher forms is simply the unfolding of pre-existing germs, and not due to evolution by modification, nor to the appearance of new lower forms by Abiogenesis. Why does not Evolution produce animals wholly unfit for their environment? This difficulty is met by Bonnet's assumption that as the whole future life was predetermined, so is the whole order of the inorganic Universe. There can, therefore, be no possibility of an animal or plant appearing out of its proper environment.

Bonnet belonged to the cataclysmic school, believing that the globe had been the scene of great revolutions, and that the chaos described by Moses was the closing chapter of one of these; thus, the Creation described in Genesis may be only a resurrection of animals previously existing. Bonnet formulated his *échelle* or scale in a manner which suggests, not the branching system of Lamarck, but the continuous links of a chain in which the higher types are simply connected with the lower in direct continuity. It is the old scale of Aristotle enlarged and defined by more modern terminology.

J. B. RENÉ ROBINET (1735-1820) was another of the speculative group. In his two works, — *De la Nature*, published in 1766, and *Considérations Philosophiques sur la gradation naturelle des formes de l'être*, published in 1768, — he advances a remarkable evolutionary structure. He denies all distinction between the organic and inorganic, and reaches an '*échelle des êtres*,' which embraces all things. Influenced by Leibnitz' law of Continuity, he supposes that Nature has an aim or constant tendency towards the perfection of each type; since the beginning her aim has been to produce Man, and the higher apes appear as the last efforts of Nature before she succeeded in making Man. It is unnecessary to add that Robinet was a daring speculator. He claimed that one's first steps should be guided by facts, but that beyond this, man's reason and intelligence should not be trammelled by observation or by experiment, but should advance free from induction.

Robinet sees in man the *chef-d'œuvre* of Nature. All the variations exhibited in the lower forms of animals, from the original prototype upwards, are to be regarded as so many trials which Nature meditates upon; not only the orang-outang, but the horse, the dog, even minerals and fossils, — are not these experiments of Nature? But man is for the time only the last of the series, for beings more perfect may replace him at any time. Robinet departs so early from observation to hypothesis, that he may be placed as one of the most extreme and irrational of this group. His work, *De la Nature*, is one of the greatest curiosities of natural history literature; he gives a long and serious catalogue of stones and other inorganic objects which bear accidental and remote resemblances to the various bodily organs of man and the lower animals. These are figured and seriously described, together with monsters of various kinds, and mermaids well authenticated, as some of the early trials of Nature in the attempt to produce man.

In one of his general principles Robinet was sound. Like Leibnitz and unlike Bonnet and De Maillet, he was a uniformitarian. Nature, he says, never advances by leaps. He applies this, however, to the origin of life, and says there is no break between the organic and inorganic. The law of Continuity applies to germs of inanimate as well as of animate matter,— these germs are capable of developing into every possible form; thus, all matter is living and there is only one kingdom,— the Animal Kingdom. The germs develop from the simplest to the most complex, and animals thus arising form a continuous chain of beings, of which the first link is a prototype of the utmost simplicity. Germs, we see, being infinitely small and placed far beyond the reach of experimental affirmation or denial, are the favourite field of the speculations of all these philosophers.

There is no idea of filiation or of Evolution in the true sense in Robinet's system of a gradual change of a lower form into a higher; all the lower, intermediate, and higher forms are held to be the direct products of the germs of Nature. In sexual reproduction, for example, the two parents do not produce these germs, but are simply the bearers of them, and generation consists merely in placing these germs under circumstances in which they can develop.

LORENZO OKEN [1] (1776–1851) approached the problems of life with certain preconceived notions of how things ought to be; as half philosopher, half

[1] Oken was born at Baden and was educated at Wurtzburg; was later Professor in the University of Zürich.

naturalist, it is evident that most of his conclusions were reached purely *a priori*. Haeckel extravagantly writes in his praise that "no doctrine approaches so nearly to the natural theory of descent as that contained in Oken's much-decried *Natur Philosophie.*" Yet in his cellular conception of the primordial forms of life, Oken was, in part, anticipated by Buffon, by the elder Darwin and by Lamarck; as has been said in his sea-slime theory, he follows so primitive a naturalist as Anaximander; and in judging of his supposed anticipation of the cell doctrine of Schleiden and Schwann, we must keep in mind the stress that is laid throughout all his philosophy upon the spherical form of his metaphysical 'All.' The skull, for example, he believed to be one of these manifestations of the archetypal sphere; it is not surprising that he conceived the cell as a sphere.

There is thus room for wide differences of opinion about Oken; his writings are such compounds of apparent sense and actual nonsense, that only by selecting and putting together certain favourably read passages, can we accord him the rank Haeckel claims for him as a prophet, whereas if we review as a whole his elements of 'physio-philosophy,' it appears that his prophecies of one page are capable upon the following page of interpretation as the vaguest speculations and absurdities. He published his outline of the *Philosophie der Natur* in 1802, in the same year in which Lamarck and Treviranus independently outlined their theories of Biology and Evolution. Oken's work is certainly not to be mentioned in the same breath with theirs, from the modern standpoint. His work upon Generation — *Die Zeugung* — appeared in 1805, containing his *Ur-Schleim* (? protoplasm) and vesicular cell theory. His " Manual of the Philosophy of Nature" appeared in 1809, in the same year with Lamarck's *Philosophie Zoologique*; again Oken suffers severely by comparison. Lamarck's is a work of science, Oken's is a tissue of speculation. In estimating Oken further, we must remember that he is a follower of the school of Schelling, and that Schelling's method was to rapidly abandon scientific induction for deduction, and to pass to the interpretation of Nature from a subjective standpoint. Oken's writings show that he was consistent in this method, and Erdmann recalls that Oken's conversion of the whole of philosophy into the philosophy of Nature is a carrying out of what Schelling merely touched upon.

It is the famous *Ur-Schleim* doctrine, in which Oken's admirers read notions of the original protoplasmic and cellular basis of all life, and in which it is said he saw the fundamental substance out of which by differentiation life has arisen.[1] " Every organic thing has arisen out of slime, and is nothing but slime in different forms. This primitive slime originated in the sea, from inorganic matter,

[1] These quotations are from Tulk's translation, the *Elements of Physiophilosophy*, published in 1847.

in the course of planetary evolution. The origin of life (*generatio originaria*) occurred upon the shores, where water, air, and earth were joined." The *Ur-Schleim* assumed the form of microscopically minute bladders, and Nature has for its unit an infinity of these. Each of these bladders has an outer dense envelope and a fluid internal content. This 'infusorium,' as he calls it, has the form of a sphere, and is developed in the following manner: it is first an aggregate of an almost infinite number of organic points; as the result of the oxydizing process, the original fluid form is replaced by a vesicle with a flowing interior and firm periphery; in this are united the three life processes of feeding, digestion, and respiration. The whole organic world consists of infusoria, and both plants and animals are simply its modifications.

Generation, according to Oken, is the synthesis or bringing together of organic spheres; as with Robinet, it is the synthesis of germs, and with Maupertuis and Diderôt, the synthesis of particles. Like the Greeks, Oken imagined that the combination of these infinitely numerous mucous points or infusoria, composed of carbon mixed in equal quantities with water and air, found its most favourable conditions at the junction of sea and land. "All life," he says, "is from the sea; the whole sea is alive. Love arose out of sea-foam." In one passage, he says: "If new individuals originate, they could not originate directly from others, but they must be resolved into the *Ur-Schleim.*" A few pages further on he offers his hypothesis of the origin of man, which is entirely inconsistent with any form of cell doctrine, when he says: "Man also is the offspring of some warm and gentle seashore, and probably rose in India, where the first peaks appeared above the waters. A certain mingling of water, of blood warmth, and of atmosphere, must have conjoined for his production; and this may have happened only once and at one spot." When we consider that this was allowed to stand in a work translated in 1847, long after Buffon's, E. Darwin's, and Lamarck's speculations upon the origin of man had been published, it shows that Oken was not only a Greek survival as a thinker, but that he entirely ignored the contemporary progress of science in France and England. In another passage he says, entirely oblivious as well of his *Ur-Schleim* as of his previous statements: "Man has not been created, but developed, so the Bible itself teaches us. God did not make man out of nothing, but took an elemental body then existing — an earth-clod or carbon; moulded it into form, thus making use of water; and breathed into it life — namely, air — whereby galvanism or the vital process arose."

The Great Naturalists.

The first of the great naturalists, Linnæus and Buffon, were born, only four days apart, early in the eighteenth century, or eighty-one years after the death of Bacon.

In the environment of the idea of Evolution, LINNÆUS (1707-1778) may be considered not as a positive but as one of the negative factors, as founding the 'school of facts' of which Cuvier was later the distinguished leader. Linnæus had been preceded as a systematist by Wotton in 1552, one of the last of the Aristotelian zoölogists; by Gessner of the same period, and one of the first zoölogists who shook off the traditions of Aristotle; by Aldrovandi in 1599; by Sperling in 1661; and by Ray, who first clearly pointed out the two criteria of a species, as permanence of form and appearance, and non-fertility with other species. Ray was followed by a number of dry, descriptive writers, who worked upon the larger groups of animals and plants. Finally the turning-point to modern Zoölogy and Botany was marked by the great work of Linnæus, the *Systema Naturæ*. The binary system of nomenclature therein proposed was a mere tool for the expression of his broad conceptions of the relation of animals and plants to each other. Species were in his mind the units of direct Creation; each species bore the impression of the thought of the Creator, not only in its external form but in its anatomical structure, its faculties, its functions; and the end of classification was to consider all these facts and to arrange animals in a *natural system* according to their greater or less likeness.

Linnæus thus took a broad view of the true basis of classification upon general structure, a view which was expanded and developed by Cuvier. As Perrier observes in his admirable critique of Linnæus, he adopted the aphorism of Leibnitz *natura non facit saltum*; to him every species was exactly intermediate between two others: " We reckon as many species as issued in pairs from the hands of the Creator." These were his earlier views in all his writings between 1735 and 1751, in which the sentence *nullæ speciæ novæ* recurs, expressing his idea of the absolute fixity of species from the period of their creation as described in Genesis, the only change being that of the extension in numbers, not of variation in kind. Yet Linnæus was too close an observer to continue to hold this idea of absolute fixity, and in 1762 we find his views had somewhat altered, and this is of particular interest because of the hypothesis which he advanced to explain the origin of new species: " All the species of one genus constituted at first (that is, at the Creation) one species, *ab initio unam constituerint speciem;* they were subsequently multiplied by hybrid generation, that is, by intercrossing with other species." He was thus inclined to admit a great increase of species, more or less recent in origin, arising by hybridity, and losing their perfection of type. He elsewhere suggested that degeneration was the result of the influences of climate or environment.

In the last and thoroughly revised edition of the *Systema Naturæ*, which appeared in 1766, we no longer find this fundamental proposition of his earlier works, *nullæ speciæ novæ*. This change of view was, however, of a very mild character in comparison with the very radical views as to the mutability of species which Buffon was expressing about the same time. The influence of Linnæus was vast; far greater than that of Buffon among his contemporaries. The two men were compared to the disadvantage of the latter, and Buffon has been charged with jealousy of the great Swede. The reason why the works of Linnæus were more influential is obvious; his system was adapted to the general state of knowledge in his day, while the ideas of Buffon were in advance of his day, and incapable of proof in the existing stage of knowledge.

GEORGE LOUIS LECLERC BUFFON (1707–1788) may be called the naturalist founder of the modern applied form of the Evolution theory. It is true that his conception of the range of Evolution changed during three periods of his life; that it is difficult to gather from his conflicting statements exactly what his opinions were, yet he laid the basis of modern Evolution in Zoölogy and Botany. We claim this for him, because he first pointed out, on a broad scale, the mutability of species in relation to changes of environment. Moreover, he advanced beyond the Greek and philosophical evolutionists, in first working out a definite theory of the causes of mutability. His writings, which cover the widest range of subjects, from Cosmogony down to some of the minutiæ of Zoölogy, undoubtedly exercised a great influence in England and in Europe. He sowed the seed of suggestion in some passages, which, it is true, were mostly speculative, and these seeds germinated in the minds of the later German Natural Philosophers, and among Buffon's contemporary naturalists, while ripening and bearing fruit in his successor, Lamarck, and others, both in France and England. Buffon's suggestiveness was one of his chief merits. It sprang from an imagination which Didérôt eulogized: " Heureux le philosophe systématique à qui la Nature aura donné comme autrefois à Epicure, à Lucrèce, à Aristôte, à Platon, une imagination forte. . . ." This imagination made and unmade Buffon, for it touched alike his soundest and unsoundest speculations.

In his early period Buffon shared the views of Linnæus, his contemporary, and it is interesting to contrast these two great men, — one the founder of the view of Classification as a fixed system of the divine order of things, and the *ne plus ultra* of Botany and Zoölogy — the other the founder of the directly opposed view of Classification as an invention of man, and of the laws governing the relations of animals and their environment as the chief end of science.] In an early edition of Buffon's *Histoire Naturelle*, we find him using almost the exact words of Linnæus: "In animals, species are separated by a gap which Nature cannot bridge over.... We see him, the Creator, dictating his simple but beautiful laws and impressing upon each species its immutable characters."

Krause points out that as early as 1755 (*Histoire Naturelle*, tome v. pp. 103, 104) Buffon found in comparative anatomy many difficulties in the Special Creation theory. "The pig," he says, "does not appear to have been formed upon an original, special, and perfect plan, since it is a compound of other animals; it has evidently useless parts, or rather parts of which it cannot make any use, toes all the bones of which are perfectly formed, and which, nevertheless, are of no service to it. Nature is far from subjecting herself to final causes in the formation of her creatures." In always looking for a purpose or design in every part, he continues, "We fail to see that we thus deprive philosophy of its true character, and misrepresent its object, which consists in the knowledge of the 'how' of things, the way in which Nature acts...." This thought was reiterated by Goethe.

In 1761 we find that he had advanced to a belief in the frequent mutability of species: "How many species, being ('*dénaturées*') perfected or degenerated by the great changes in land and sea, by the favours or disfavours of Nature, by food, by the prolonged influences of climate, contrary or favourable, *are no longer what they formerly were.*" Again he says: " One is surprised at the rapidity with which species vary, and the facility with which they lose their primitive characteristics in assuming new forms."

We are tempted to translate the term '*dénaturées*' by our modern term 'evolved,' since, as we see above, Buffon embraced in it the two modern ideas of development ('*perfectionnement*') and degeneration ('*dégeneration*'). But this would convey a broader conception than seems to have been at any time in his mind; for, by the express use of '*dénaturées*,' he gives us an insight into the limits of his conception. He could not wholly shake off the idea that each species was originally a special type, as impressed by the Creator, containing some ineffaceable and permanent characters, and that variation consisted in the departure from these natural and original characters. Thus he was deeply impressed with the fixity of type impression among the larger animals, such as the quadrupeds, believing them to be comparatively invariable. Throughout Buffon's writings we find this wavering between the science of Genesis and the evidence of zoölogy. It is sometimes expressed in paragraphs which closely follow one another, wherein it is difficult to decide whether Buffon is ironical or not. Referring, in one instance, to his idea of unity of type, he seems to indicate that, in creating animals, the Supreme Being only employed a single idea, and at the same time varied it in every possible manner; passing on to the unity of type which pervades certain families, he says, in effect: If we reason out this matter, we find that the fundamental idea of the family is community of origin for the man and the ape, as well as for the horse and the ass. The ass is a degenerate horse; the ape is a degenerate man. In carrying this back to its logical extreme, we are forced to admit that these animals sprang from a common source, — from one animal, which, in the succession of time, has produced by perfecting itself (*se perfectionnant*), and by degeneration, all the races of other animals. But no, he continues (whether seriously or not it is hard to say), it is certain by Revelation that all animals have shared the benefits of direct creation, and have issued, completely formed, pair by pair, from the hands of the Creator.

"... Mais non: il est certain, par la révélation, que tous les animaux ont également participé à la grâce de la création; que les deux premiers de chaque espèce, et de toutes les espèces, sont sortis tout formés des mains du Créateur; et l'on doit croire qu'ils étaient tels à peu près qu'ils nous sont aujourd'hui représentés par leurs descendants."

It is this wavering of opinion and this change from earlier to later views which has led different writers to hold such widely different opinions as to Buffon's share in the development of the Evolution idea. M. de Lanessan claims for him the position which is usually accorded to Lamarck; and, on the other hand, other writers, such as Isidore St. Hilaire and Haeckel, assign him a much less important position. St. Hilaire shows clearly that his opinions marked three periods. Quatrefages hardly realizes the great influence exerted by the writings of Buffon's middle period, when his views were most extreme. Lanessan, his greatest admirer, believes that he has anticipated not only Lamarck in his conception of the action of environment, but Darwin in the struggle for existence and Survival of the Fittest. There is no doubt that in some passages Buffon doubted not only the fixity, but even the reality of species, genera, families, and other taxonomic divisions; also that he wrote of the chain of organic life from the zoöphytes to the monkeys and man, thus borrowing from Aristotle and suggestive of Bonnet and his famous scale.

Buffon's ideas regarding the physical basis of heredity are very similar to those of Democritus, and certainly contain the basis of the conception of the Pangenesis theory of Darwin, for he supposes that the elements of the germ-cells were gathered from all parts of the body. He does not expressly speak of the transmission of acquired characters as a logical part of his theory of heredity, but such transmission was undoubtedly in his mind, although not clearly formulated as by Lamarck.

He illustrates the direct influences of environment in the changes observed in the different races of men as connected with differences of climate. He carefully traces the modifications which are due to the domestication of various wild animals. He speaks of the formation of new varieties of animals by artificial selection, and shows that similar results may be produced in Nature by geographical migration, thus having in mind the 'segregation' law, later developed by Wagner.

The struggle for existence, the elimination of the least-perfected species, the contest between the fecundity of certain species and their constant destruction, are all clearly expressed in various passages. Thus we find Buffon anticipating Malthus[1] in the following passage: —

"Le cours ordinaire de la nature vivante, est en général toujours constant, toujours le même ; son mouvement, toujours régulier, roule sur deux points inébranlables : l'un, la fécondité sans bornes donnée à toutes les espèces ; l'autre, les obstacles sans nombre qui réduisent cette fécondité à une mesure déterminée et ne laissent en tout temps qu'à peu près la même quantité d'individus de chaque espèce."

Again, his idea of the elimination of the least-perfected species is shown in the following passage, also quoted by De Lanessan: —

"Les espèces les moins parfaites, les plus délicates, les plus pesantes, les moins agissantes, les moins armées, etc., ont déjà disparu or disparaîtront."

[1] Thomas Robert Malthus (1766-1834) published his famous work, *An Essay on the Principle of Population as it affects the Future Improvement of Society*, in 1798, while Buffon made the last addition to his *Histoire Naturelle* in 1789. As another instance of continuity it is interesting to recall the obligation Darwin expresses to Malthus.

Buffon not only saw the negative influences of environment in the reduction of numbers and in the reduction of imperfect types, but also its positive action in the production of new characters, and here we come upon the third and main feature of what may be called his theory of the factors of Evolution; namely, the direct action of environment in the modification of the structure of animals and plants and the conservation of these modifications through heredity. He applied this factor to the origin of new species in the New World of America. It is amusing to the modern zoölogist to note that Buffon, in common with all his contemporaries, always conceived of the New World as not only new in point of discovery, but as new in its zoölogical evolution. He illustrated his ideas as to the direct action of environment in saying that Old-World types, finding their way into the New World, would there undergo modifications sufficient to cause us to regard them as new species; and in this connection Buffon expresses the uniformitarian idea which Lamarck carried to such an extreme (which was opposed to his general cataclysmal teaching, that Nature is in a continual state of transition); namely, that man must consider and observe changes which are going on in his own period in order to understand what has gone on in the past, and what will happen in the future.

It is with such passages as these that Buffon inspired later writers to consider the great problem.

He may be said, to have asked all the questions which were to be answered in the course of the succeeding century. It is in this suggestiveness that we find his chief merits. As St. Hilaire says, his glory lies in what he prepared for his successors, in his creation of a philosophy of Comparative Zoölogy, his views of community of origin, laws of geographical distribution, extinction of old species, and successive apparition of new species. In order to be fair to Buffon's followers, we must further test the breadth of his conception by his application of it to the succession of life; and we here find in numerous passages, as pointed out by Quatrefages, that his conception was very limited.

After having maintained in his first period the extreme Special Creation view, and in his second period, especially between 1761 and 1766, the extreme transmutation view, he returned finally to the moderate view, that species were neither fixed nor mutable, but that specific types could assume a great variety of forms.

In his theory of Evolution, considering temperature, climate, food, and capillarity as the three causes of change, alteration, and degeneration of animals, he does not employ the terms heredity or transmission of acquired characters, although it is evident that these factors are implied. In other words, Quatrefages points out, Buffon did not follow his theory into its details.

He also failed to reach the phyletic or branching

idea of Evolution. He expressly says that the relations of species furnish a problem beyond our reach: —

"Nous ne pourrions nous prononcer plus affirmativement si les limites qui séparent les espèces, ou la chaîne qui les unit, nous étaient mieux connues; mais qui peut avoir suivi la grande filiation de toutes les généalogies dans la nature? Il faut être né avec elle et avoir pour ainsi dire, des observations contemporaines."

Buffon thus left untouched many problems for his successors, Erasmus Darwin, Lamarck, and Goethe.

ERASMUS DARWIN (1731-1802), grandfather of the great naturalist, is one of the most interesting figures in our present history. In his volumes of verse we find that he is one of the poets of the Evolution idea, following Empedocles and Lucretius, and followed by the greater poet Goethe. In the *Temple of Nature*, published after his death, in the year 1802 memorable for coincidences, he gives in poetical form the ideas which had matured during the last ten years of his life. His earlier writings were the *Botanic Garden* and *Loves of the Plants*, two volumes of verse completed and published about 1788, and his *Zoonomia*, a large medico-philosophical work published in 1794.

We owe to Dr. Ernst Krause a careful study of the works of Erasmus Darwin, originally published in *Kosmos*, and subsequently republished in English, with a biography of Erasmus Darwin written by Charles Darwin. Krause has selected from the *Temple of Nature* many verses showing Dr. Darwin's views of Evolution, and opening with his belief in the Greek doctrine of the spontaneous origin of life, which we have seen revived during the eighteenth century in so many extravagant forms, but which Dr. Darwin restricts to the lowest organisms:

> " Hence without parents, by spontaneous birth,
> Rise the first specks of animated earth.
> . . . .
> Organic life beneath the shoreless waves
> Was born and nurs'd in ocean's pearly caves;
> First, forms minute, unseen by spheric glass,
> Move on the mud, or pierce the watery mass;
> These, as successive generations bloom,
> New powers acquire and larger limbs assume;
> Whence countless groups of vegetation spring,
> And breathing realms of fin and feet and wing."

Then, in the transition from sea to dry land, came the amphibious, and finally the terrestrial forms of life. Gradually new powers are acquired. In these metamorphoses, Dr. Darwin does not revive the fancies of such writers as De Maillet, but illustrates his views by changes such as those seen in the development from the tadpole to the frog. Passing on, he speaks of cross-fertilization, and finally reaches the origin of Man. We here find a very interesting section. Dr. Darwin quotes Buffon and Helvetius to the effect that many features in the anatomy of man point to a former quadrupedal position, and indicate that he is not yet fully adapted to the erect position; that, further, Man may have arisen from a single family of monkeys (we here suppose the family is used in the ordinary sense), in which, accidentally, the opposing muscle brought the thumb against the tips of the fingers, and that this muscle gradually increased in size by use in successive generations.[1] Thus, Darwin calls our attention to Buffon's anticipation of the Natural Selection idea as applied to man, in the *survival of an accidental variation* in a muscle of the greatest importance in the history of man.

Dr. Darwin devotes a whole canto to the human hand.

> "The hand, first gift of Heaven! to man belongs;
> Untipt with claws, the circling fingers close,
> With rival points the bending thumbs oppose,
> Trace the nice lines of Form with sense refined,
> And clear ideas charm the thinking mind."

He passes on to outline the development of the human faculties. Later he describes the fierce struggle for existence, in verses which remind us of Tennyson's lines upon Nature, red in tooth and claw. Not only do animals destroy each other and plants,

---

[1] This recalls the modern parody: —

> "There was an ape in days that were earlier;
> Centuries passed and his hair became curlier;
> Centuries more and his thumb gave a twist,
> And he was a man and a Positivist."

but even the plants struggle among themselves for soil, moisture, air, and light, and he connects this with the idea which we have already seen expressed by Buffon and Malthus, that this struggle checks the naturally rapid increase of life, and thus is advantageous and beneficial in the end. As Dr. Krause points out, Darwin just misses the connection between this struggle and the Survival of the Fittest.

These passages show that Dr. Darwin was at the last — that is in his latest writings — a firm evolutionist, and that he had advanced considerably beyond the tentative views expressed many years before in the *Zoonomia* and *Botanic Garden*. Krause, in his admirable biography, does not, however, give Darwin's predecessors sufficient credit; his ideas, it is true, were largely gathered from his own notes as a physician and as a lifelong observer of Nature, but they indicate also a very careful reading of Leibnitz, as in his allusion to the change of genera in the Ammonites; to Buffon, as in ideas connected with the struggle for existence and variations under artificial selection; to Linnæus, Blumenthal, and others. As to the origin of life, he drew from the Greeks, especially from Aristotle, limiting spontaneous generation, however, to the lowest organisms; they also gave him the fundamental idea of Evolution, for he says, "This idea of the gradual formation and improvement of the Animal world seems not to have been unknown to the ancient philosophers." His general philosophy of Nature, as under the operation of natural laws rather than of the supernatural, he himself in the *Zoonomia* attributes to David Hume.

Dr. Darwin's theory of the causes of Evolution was not similar to Buffon's, for he nowhere lays stress upon the modifications induced by the direct action of Environment; on the other hand, he believed that modifications spring from within by the reactions of the organism; thus he fully anticipated what is now known as the Lamarckian theory, and extended it even further than Lamarck, since he endowed plants with sensibility and attributed their evolution to their own efforts towards the attainment of certain structures. His view of the origin of adaptations or of design in Nature was thoroughly naturalistic, believing that adaptations had not been specially created, but that they had been naturally and gradually acquired by powers of development planted within the original organisms by the Creator.

In a defence of Lamarck's originality, Quatrefages mistakenly attributes to Dr. Darwin the theory of an 'inherent perfecting tendency'; but this we find is an entire misconception. Let us, therefore, carefully examine Dr. Darwin's theory as expounded in the chapter 'Generation' of the *Zoonomia*. In this chapter he combats Bonnet's doctrine of *emboîtement*, and defends the idea of individual development by successive additions of parts to the embryo. In the original formation of the embryo he rejects the Pangenesis theory of Buffon, that is, of the conjugation of like parts from the two parents. "These organic particles, he (Mr. Buffon) supposes to exist in the spermatic fluids of both sexes, and that they are derived thither from every part of the body, and must therefore resemble, as he supposes, the parts from whence they are derived." He substitutes for this a theory of his own, of the addition of parts, which takes little account of the laws of heredity.

The individual life begins, as all life originally began, from a single filament. "Shall we conjecture," he says, "that one and the same kind of living filament is and has been the cause of all organic life? ... I suppose this living filament, of whatever form it may be, whether sphere, cube, or cylinder, to be endowed with the capability of being excited into action by certain kinds of stimulus." This irritability and excitability is the first step in Darwin's conception of Evolution. It is that whereby animals and plants react to their environment, causing changes in their own structure, and these changes are transmitted to their offspring.

In this chapter upon Generation, he throws out a wealth of suggestion and inquiry which indicates a thorough appreciation of the problems which were yet to be solved, as well as of the broadest aspects of Evolution. He touches upon Embryology, Comparative Anatomy, the Colouring of

Animals, Artificial Selection, and treats Environment almost in its broadest sense. We may briefly follow the outline of his argument for Evolution in the *Zoonomia*. He says:—

"When we revolve in our minds the metamorphoses of animals, as from the tadpole to the frog; secondly, the changes produced by artificial cultivation, as in the breeds of horses, dogs, and sheep; thirdly, the changes produced by conditions of climate and of season, as in the sheep of warm climates being covered with hair instead of wool, and the hares and partridges of northern climates becoming white in winter: when, further, we observe the changes of structure produced by habit, as seen especially in men of different occupations; or the changes produced by artificial mutilation and prenatal influences, as in the crossing of species and production of monsters; fourth, when we observe the essential unity of plan in all warm-blooded animals, — we are led to conclude that they have been alike produced from a similar living filament."

Having thus discussed some of the most obvious arguments for mutability, he proceeds to speculate upon the causes of these changes. "Fifthly," he says, "all animals undergo transformations which are in part produced by their own exertions, in response to pleasures and pains, *and many of these acquired forms or propensities are transmitted to their posterity.*"

This, so far as I know, is the first clear and definite statement of the theory of the transmission of acquired characters considered as one of the factors of Evolution. We will now continue to examine Darwin's argument, and later will illustrate his application of his theory. He proceeds to discuss the wants of animals, arranging them first under the head of sexual characters, as horns, spurs, developed for purposes of combat and procuring the females. Thus, the horns of the stag have not been developed to protect him from the boar, but from other stags. He here misses the idea of the sexual selection of the horns developed as ornaments to the male. Other organs, he says, are developed in the search for food. Cattle have acquired rough tongues to pull off the blades of grass; and of these and similar organs he says: "All which seem to have been gradually produced during many generations, by the perpetual endeavour of the creatures to supply the want of food, and to have been delivered to their posterity with constant improvements for the purpose required." Again he says: "There are organs developed for protective purposes, diversifying both the form and colour of the body for concealment and for combat." He here definitely unfolds the idea of protective colouring.

He closes his long argument by pointing out the close gradations in Nature from the higher to the lower forms, and the substantial similarity between the animal and vegetable kingdoms in their modes of generation or reproduction, and concludes as follows:—

"From thus meditating upon the minute portion of time in which many of the above changes have been produced, would it be too bold to imagine, in the great length of time since the earth began to exist, perhaps millions of ages before the commencement of the history of mankind, that all warm-blooded animals have arisen from one living filament, which the first great Cause imbued with animality, with the power of acquiring new parts, attended with new propensities, directed by irritations, sensations, volitions, and associations, and thus possessing the faculty of continuing to improve by its own inherent activity, and of delivering down those improvements by generation to posterity, world without end?"

We must remember in reading this sentence that by generation Darwin means inheritance, heredity being a term which was introduced much later. If we analyze this sentence, we see that it involves, first, a clear idea of the evolution of all forms of life from a single filament or minute organic mass, as we should express it to-day, — a minute mass of protoplasm; second, that this evolution has occupied millions of years and has been controlled not by supernatural causes but by natural causes. The directing power to which he alludes has sprung from its efforts to meet its new needs in course of its changing environment. For it is clear from the context that by the term 'inherent activity,' Darwin does not allude to an automatic perfecting principle such as we find originated with Aristotle, but that the power of improvement rests with the animal's own efforts, the effects of these efforts upon the body being transmitted. Darwin seems to feel that he may be charged with irreverence in thus substituting the idea of Evolution for that of Special Creation; he meets this by establishing his hypothesis upon a basis of natural causation or secondary causes, and says: —

"For if we may compare infinities, it would seem to require a greater infinity or power to cause the causes of effects, than to cause the effects themselves; that is, to establish the laws of Creation rather than to directly create."

There are many single passages which further illustrate Darwin's ideas. It is first, perfectly clear that he derives all forms of life from a single filament, which we may translate into a single protoplasmic mass. Upon this, however, he does not build a branching or phyletic system of Evolution, but simply leaves this part of the system out, and passes on to illustrations of the causes and laws of Evolution. As pointed out above, his fundamental idea is what has since been called 'Archæsthetism' by Cope. According to this, growth is stimulated by irritability and sensibility, or in Darwin's language — in the passage upwards from the original filament: "The most essential parts of the system are first formed by the irritations (of hunger, thirst, etc., above mentioned) and by the pleasurable sensations attending those irritations, and by exertions in consequence of painful sensations, similar to those of hunger and suffocation.... In confirmation of these ideas, it may be observed that all parts of the body endeavour to grow or to make additional parts of themselves throughout our lives.' (*Zoonomia*, XXXIX. 3.)

I have carefully searched for these passages, and find a most striking confirmation of Charles Darwin's well-known sentence: "It is curious how largely my grandfather, Dr. Erasmus Darwin, anticipated the views and erroneous grounds of opinion of Lamarck in his *Zoonomia*." Among the passages above quoted, and in those following, we find the whole framework and even in part the very language of Lamarck's Four Laws.

Dr. Darwin again illustrates his theory, speaking of the Evolution of Man:—

"Now as labour strengthens the muscles employed and increases their bulk, it would seem that a few generations of labour or indolence may in this respect change the form and temperament of the body." (*Zoonomia*, pp. 356, 501.) "Add to these the various changes produced in the forms of mankind by their early modes of exertion . . . which became hereditary."

On the following page he applies the law of transmission of acquired characters to the lower animals. After speaking of the snout of the pig, the trunk of the elephant, the rough tongues of cattle, and beaks of birds, he says:—

"All which seem to have been gradually produced during many generations by the perpetual endeavour of the creatures to supply the want of food, and to have been delivered to their posterity with constant improvement of them for the purposes acquired."

As regards the origin of plants, he at one point mentions the suggestion of Linnæus: "And that from thence, as Linnæus has conjectured in respect to the vegetable world, it is not impossible but the great variety of species of animals which now tenant the earth, may have had their origin from the mixture of a few natural orders." Elsewhere he speaks of plants as having arisen in the contest for light and air. He carries the idea of sensibility and irritability into plant life, and his theory of plant evolution is similar to that of animal evolution.

Erasmus Darwin was, however, fully conscious of the limitations of his theory of Evolution; for in speaking of protective colouring (p. 510), he says: "The final cause of these colours is readily understood, as they serve some purpose of the animal, but the efficient cause would seem almost beyond conjecture." The same question we have seen propounded by Kant at about the same period: "How can purposeful forms of organization arise without a purposeful working cause? How can a work full of design build itself up without a design and without a builder?" Of course we do not know whether Darwin had this suggested to him by Kant, but it is exceedingly interesting to see him so clearly state the old, old problem which his grandson later largely solved.

While this chapter on Generation is a comparatively small part of the *Zoonomia*, we learn that it attracted much attention at the time. Dr. McCosh tells the writer that he read the work while in Edinburgh. It made a considerable sensation, and was replied to by Thomas Brown, M.D. This reply, together with his article upon " Cause and Effect," won for Dr. Brown the professorship of Moral Philosophy in the University. We see, therefore, that in England, as we shall see in France, the adherents of the Evolution doctrine found the spirit of the Universities hostile; and as we pass from man to man in these outlines of the Evolution idea, selecting certain paragraphs and ignoring all the contemporary literature, we must not lose sight of the fact that the major weight of opinion was, throughout all this period, upon the side of Special Creation. For one argument like Dr. Darwin's upon the gradual development side, there were hundreds upon the side of sudden production.

V.

FROM LAMARCK TO ST. HILAIRE.

Ainsi, la nature, toujours agissante, toujours impassible, renouvelant et variant toute espèce de corps, n'en préservant aucun de la destruction, nous offre une scène imposante et sans terme, et nous montre en elle une puissance particulière qui n'agit que par nécessité. — LAMARCK.

WE have now come to an important step in the history of the Evolution theory; that is, the relation of Erasmus Darwin to Lamarck. We shall see, in treating Lamarck, that the parallelism between the line of reasoning of these two men is very striking. They not only used the same illustrations, but almost the same language; and by putting together various passages from Darwin's writings, we can reconstruct, almost verbatim, the four principles of Lamarck. Darwin's work was published in 1794 while as Huxley points out, in his *Recherches sur les causes des principaux faits physiques*, written in 1776, but not published until 1794, Lamarck adopted Buffon's maturer and more conservative views, as shown in the following sentence: —

All the individuals of this nature are derived from similar individuals, which altogether constitute the entire species. . . . If there exist many varieties produced by the action of environment, these varieties do not degenerate to the point of forming new species. . . .

It was not until 1801, seven years after the publication of the *Zoonomia*, that Lamarck published his theory of the mutability of species, and this theory had two main features, namely, that animals were evolved, not, as Buffon supposed, by the direct external action of environment, but by environment acting upon internal structure through the nervous system, and by the transmission of the modifications thus produced. As regards the origin of plants, Lamarck believed with Buffon, that they were evolved by the direct action of environment. Lamarck nowhere makes any allusion to the *Zoonomia*, and De Lanessan has pointed out that he also pays a very scant tribute to Buffon, while there is the strongest internal evidence that Lamarck was largely influenced by the writings of Buffon's second period.

How shall we explain this coincidence or apparent plagiarism? We must adopt one of two alternatives. One is, as later in the famous and quite as closely parallel Wallace-Darwin case, that both naturalists arrived independently at the same conclusions, influenced alike by the writings of Linnæus and Buffon and by their own observations upon Nature; or, we must suppose that Lamarck borrowed freely from Darwin without giving him credit. We should hesitate before adopting the latter alternative, when we consider that the interchange of thought between the two countries was not as constant as at present, also that Dr. Darwin's views were buried rather obscurely in a great quarto mainly devoted to medicine, and in two long didactic poems. Again, we must note that Geoffroy St-

Hilaire, while crediting Goethe, Buffon, and others with having partly anticipated Lamarck, and giving a very complete bibliographical description of the subject, nowhere mentions Erasmus Darwin. It does not seem probable that Darwin's work could have been used by Lamarck, and have remained wholly unknown to St. Hilaire. The dates and the points of internal evidence still seem to justify the suggestion of Charles Darwin, and the very strong suspicion of Dr. Krause, that Lamarck was familiar with the *Zoonomia*, and made use of it in the development of his theory.

M. Ch. Martins, the biographer of Lamarck, calls attention to the fact that Laplace supported Lamarck in the doctrine of the inheritance of acquired habits, as applied to the origin of the mental faculties of man; and in the passages quoted by Martins to sustain this point, we have evidence that both Laplace and Lamarck anticipated Spencer. We have seen that the general doctrine of transmission of acquired characters was an old one. It had been expressed in France by others, by De Maillet, for example. The most important testimony in favour of Lamarck's originality is his own. It is in a very striking passage in the introduction of the last edition of his *Animaux sans Vertèbres* (p. 2). This was Lamarck's latest work. He says:—

"I set forth my general theory. It deserves close attention; and as far as possible, men should determine how far I am well founded in all that I have written. I have, in fact, advanced a general theory upon the origin of life and upon its modes of manifestation, upon the origin of the faculties, upon the variations and phenomena of organization of different animals,—a theory consistent in its principles and applicable to all cases. *It is the first, so it seems to me, which has been presented, the only theory, therefore, which exists*, because I do not know any work which offers another theory based upon such a large number of principles and considerations. This theory of mine recognizes in Nature the power to produce some result, in fact, all the results we see. Is it well established? Certainly, it seems to me so; and all my observations tend to confirm it. Otherwise I would not publish it. It rests with those who do not accept it to substitute another, with equally wide application, or with a still wider application to the facts. But this I hardly believe to be possible."

Upon this sentence it seems that we have satisfactory evidence that Erasmus Darwin and Lamarck independently evolved their views, and this is further confirmed by a careful reading of Lamarck's first exposition of his theory in his work of 1802. This has very little similarity with Darwin's form of statement or language, although it embodies essentially the same theory. To Huxley's rather pointed question: "It would be interesting to know what was the occasion of Lamarck's change of view between 1779 and 1802?"—we may answer that this change was probably due to the change of his studies from Botany to Zoölogy, for it was upon animal life that his theory was developed.

LAMARCK.

LAMARCK (1744–1829), as the founder of the complete modern theory of Descent, is the most prominent figure between Aristotle and Darwin. One cannot compare his *Philosophie Zoologique* with all previous and contemporary contributions to the Evolution theory, or learn the extraordinary difficulties under which he laboured, and that this work was put forth only a few years after he had turned from Botany to Zoölogy, without gaining the greatest admiration for his genius. No one has been more misunderstood, or judged with more partiality by over or under praise. The stigma placed upon his writings by Cuvier, who greeted every fresh edition of his works as a '*nouvelle folie*,' and the disdainful allusions to him by Charles Darwin (the only writer of whom Darwin ever spoke in this tone), long placed him in the light of a purely extravagant, speculative thinker. Yet, as a fresh instance of the certainty with which men of science finally obtain recognition, it is gratifying to note the admiration which has been accorded to him in Germany by Haeckel and others, by his countrymen, and by a large school of American and English writers of the present day; to note, further, that his theory was finally taken up and defended by Charles Darwin himself, and that it forms the very heart of the system of Herbert Spencer.

None the less, it is now a question under discussion, whether Lamarck's factor is a factor in Evolution at all! If it prove to be no factor, Lamarck will sink gradually into obscurity as one great figure in the history of opinion. If it prove to be a real factor, he will rise into a more eminent position than he now holds, — into a rank not far below Darwin's.

Jeanne Baptiste Pierre Antoine de Monet, otherwise known as the Chevalier de Lamarck, was, according to his biographer, a man of great physical and moral courage. He distinguished himself by an act of singular bravery in the army, and, receiving an injury, re-entered life as a doctor. He was first attracted to Botany by the rich flora observed during his military service near Monaco, and, coming to Paris, he gained Buffon's attention, and became an intimate friend of his household. His *Flore Française*, written in six months, was printed under Buffon's direction, and passed through many editions. This was a systematic work, an adaptation of the system of Linnæus to the flora of France. He seems to have been gifted with exceptionally rapid observation, with great facility in writing, and with unusual powers of definition and description. At the age of forty-nine he was transferred, under the Directory, to a Zoölogical chair in the Jardins des Plantes. Lamarck was especially placed in charge of the invertebrates, and at the same time Geoffroy St. Hilaire was appointed to the care of the vertebrates. He took up the study of

Zoölogy with such zeal and success, that he almost immediately introduced striking reforms in classification. The early fruits of Lamarck's zoölogical studies were not only a series of very valuable additions to the classification of animals, such as the divisions, Vertebrata and Invertebrata, and the groups, Crustacea, Arachnida, and Annelida, but the rapid development of a true conception of the mutability of species, and of the great law of the origin of species by descent.

His devotion to the study of the small forms of life, probably with inferior facilities for work, for he was extremely poor, gradually deprived him of the use of his eyes, and in 1819 he became completely blind. The last two volumes of the first edition of his *Histoire Naturelle des Animaux sans Vertèbres*, which was begun in 1816 and completed in 1822, was carried on by dictation to his daughter, who showed him the greatest affection; after Lamarck was confined to his room, it is said she never left the house. Lamarck was thus saddened in his old age by extreme poverty and by the harsh reception of his transmutation theories, in the truth of which he felt the most absolute conviction.

The development of Lamarck's views was, as we have seen above, apparently coincident with his turning from Botany to Zoölogy. His route of observation lay along Comparative Zoölogy and Botany, as Goethe's lay along the Comparative Anatomy and Morphology of plants and animals.

It seems that the most speculative of all his writings were his earlier physical treatises. One of these early works was his *Recherches sur les causes des principaux faits physiques*, written in 1766, presented to the Academy in 1780, and published in 1794, (the date of the *Zoonomia*). Here Lamarck, as we have seen, affirms his belief in the immutability of species and strong disbelief in the theory of the spontaneous origin of life, saying that all the physical forces we know, combined, cannot form a single organic being capable of reproduction. All individuals in organic life descend from other individuals altogether similar, which taken together constitute the entire species. It is certain from this that in 1766 Lamarck held views similar to those of his master, Buffon, in his third period. It is possible that prior to 1794 his own opinions had become modified, but that he had left his original manuscript unchanged for publication.

In his *Hydrogéologie*, published in 1802, he developed his uniformitarian ideas in Geology and proposed the term 'Biology' for the sciences of life. In the same year appeared his *Recherches sur l'Organisation des Corps Vivants*, in which he first sketches out his Evolution theory. This work was particularly upon the origin of the living body, upon the causes of its development, and its progressive composition. It is in the preface of this work that he speaks of projecting a 'Physique Terrestre,' to include three parts: *Hydréologie, Météorologie*, and

Biologie. The two latter sections were never completed. It is important to note that in this work he projects a scale of life somewhat similar to that of Bonnet and of Aristotle. This shows that in his mind at that time, the history of life presented itself as a vertical chain of masses of organisms not of species; so far as appears, he had not then developed the branching idea. This chain he puts forth to show the '*dégradation*' or gradation from the highest to the lowest forms, indicating the march of Nature in its progressive developments. Here and elsewhere Lamarck acknowledges his indebtedness to the Greeks, especially to Aristotle. Two main principles are brought out in this work anticipating his later theory of the causes of Evolution: first, it is not organs which have given rise to habits, but habits, modes of life, and environment which have given rise to organs; as illustrated by the blindness of the mole, by the presence of teeth in mammals, and the absence of teeth in birds. His second principle is, that life is an order and condition of things in the parts of all bodies which possess it, which renders possible all the organic movements within.

There is no evidence in this work that Lamarck had seen Darwin's *Zoonomia*. The parallelism with the *Zoonomia* comes out much more prominently in Lamarck's most important speculative work, the *Philosophie Zoologique*, published in 1809, in which his earlier views are developed and expanded. This is characterized by a clear and beautiful style, and by a logical development of the argument, in which Lamarck's whole scheme of Evolution is gradually unfolded. His theory was never developed beyond this point, although he restated it in a more condensed form in the introduction to both editions of his *Histoire des Animaux sans Vertèbres* between 1816 and 1822.

The *Philosophie Zoologique* shows that three truths had now come to him from his labours in Botany and Zoölogy, and presumably from his wider readings of Buffon's earlier writings, of Linnæus, and of the Greeks, to whom he makes allusion. These are, first, the certainty that species vary under changing external influences; second, that there is a fundamental unity in the animal kingdom; third, that there is a progressive and perfecting development. Among the influences of environment he cites the cases of the supposed influence of water upon plants and upon the lower animals; the influence of air in forming the entire respiratory system of birds; the influence of light upon plants, directly upon the colouring of animals, and upon the development and degeneration of eyes, and the influences of heat. The main influences come under the law of Use and Disuse, for he believes that Nature does not effect her changes directly, but through the reaction of animals to their environment.

He thus differs widely from Buffon: " Lack of employment of an organ becoming constant under the influence of certain habits, gradually impoverishes the organ and ends by causing it to disappear entirely." In the *Discours préliminaire*, he outlines his work as divided into three parts. The first is to treat of the subject in general, of methods of research, of artificial distinctions raised by man in classification, of the real meaning of the term 'species,' of the proofs of the '*dégradation*' (Evolution) of organization from one end to the other of the animal scale, of the influences of environment and habit as causes favouring or arresting the development of animals, of the natural order and classification of animals. In this first section his whole theory of Evolution is to be expanded, which we will examine later. In the second part, he considers the essential phenomena and physiological conditions of life or '*orgasme*,' and irritability, of the peculiarities of cellular tissue, of the conditions of spontaneous generation. This section covers what we would now term the general principles of Biology. The third part is devoted to the development of the nervous system, sensation, action, and intelligence, including a theory of the origin and formation of the nerves, and of the development of mental faculties and ideas, lower and higher. Here he treats of the relation of the mind of man to that of the lower animals.

Lamarck's general philosophy of Nature comes forth here. He is, first of all, an advocate of the search for secondary causes, as opposed to arrest with supernatural causation. He believes that we see in Nature a certain order originally imposed by its Author, which is manifested in the successive development of life; we thus study natural forces and Nature abandoned to its laws. In this sense we see Nature creating and developing without cessation towards higher and higher types. External conditions do not alter this order of development, but give it infinite variety by directing the scale of being into an infinite number of branches. Lamarck denied, absolutely, the existence of any 'perfecting tendency' in Nature, and regarded Evolution as the final necessary effect of surrounding conditions on life. Thus, in his Teleology, he adopted the modern standpoint. Instead of suggesting that animals had been created for a certain mode of life, he supposed that their mode of life had itself created them. Wings were not given to birds to enable them to fly, but they had developed wings in attempting to fly.

In his discussion of Evolution in general, in the section, '*De l'Ordre naturel des Animaux*,' he says:—

"In considering the natural order of animals, the very positive gradation which exists in their structure, organization, and in the number as well as in the perfection of their faculties, is very far removed from being a new truth, because the Greeks themselves fully perceived it; but they were unable to expose the principles and the proofs of this evolution, because they lacked the knowledge necessary to establish it. In consideration of this gradation of life, there are only two conclusions which face us as to its origin: — *The conclusion adopted up to to-day:* Nature (or its Author) in creating animals has foreseen all possible sorts of circumstances in which they would be destined to live, and has given to each species a constant organization, as well as a form determined and invariable in its parts, which forces each species to live in the places and climates where it is found, and there to preserve the habits which we know belong to it. *My personal conclusion:* Nature, in producing successively all the species of animals, and commencing by the most imperfect or the most simple to conclude its labour in the most perfect, has gradually completed their organization; and of these animals, while spreading generally in all the habitable regions of the globe, each species has received, under the influence of environment which it has encountered, the habits which we recognize and the modifications in its parts which observation reveals in it."

The first conclusion (Special Creation), he goes on to say, is one which has been held by nearly every one up to the present time. It attributes to each animal a constancy of structure, and parts which have never varied and will never vary. To disprove the second conclusion (Evolution), he continues, it is necessary to prove, first, that each point upon the surface of the globe never varies in its nature, climate, exposure, elevation, and so forth.

The belief in the uniformity of past and present changes was the next great factor in the development of Lamarck's theory. It arose from his contemplation of the data of Geology in connection with those of Biology, as was afterwards the case with Darwin, in so marked a degree. In Geology he was an ardent advocate of the doctrine of uniformity, as against the cataclysmal school. The main principles are laid down in his *Hydrogéologie*, that all the revolutions of the earth are extremely slow. "For Nature," he says, "time is nothing. It is never a difficulty, she always has it at her disposal; and it is for her the means by which she has accomplished the greatest as well as the least of her results. For all the evolution of the earth and of living beings, Nature needs but three elements,— space, time, and matter." Lamarck, unlike Buffon, did not touch Cosmogony; but in his observations upon Geology he learnt, the first of all lessons, that in speculating upon the past we should not regard it as a period of catastrophe, that the true method of study is to observe the steady march of Nature at the present time; for its present operations suffice to explain all the facts which we observe in all its past. This led Lamarck to the extreme of denying all catastrophes in Geology, and all leaps or sudden transitions in living Nature. "Nature," he repeats, "to perfect and to diversify animals requires merely matter, space, and time."

After this review of Lamarck's self-education, intellectual equipment, and the influences of his collateral studies, we come to his theory of the factors and nature of the Evolution of life, which were first fully expressed in the *Philosophie Zoologique*, and formulated later in the *Histoire Naturelle* into the four well-known propositions : —

First Law. — Life by its internal forces tends continually to increase the volume of every body that possesses it, as well as to increase the size of all the parts of the body up to a limit which it brings about.

Second Law. — The production of a new organ or part results from a new need or want, which continues to be felt, and from the new movement which this need initiates and causes to continue. (This is the psychical factor in his theory, which Cope later has termed Archæsthetism.)

Third Law. — The development of organs and their force or power of action are always in direct relation to the employment of these organs. (At another point he expands this into two sub-laws: " In every animal which has not passed the term of its development, the more frequent and sustained employment of each organ strengthens little by little this organ, develops it, increases it in size, and gives it a power proportioned to the length of its employment; whereas the constant lack of use of the same organ insensibly weakens it, deteriorates it, progressively diminishes its powers, and ends by causing it to disappear." This is now known as the Law of Use and Disuse, or Kinetogenesis.)

Fourth Law. — All that has been acquired or altered in the organization of individuals during their life is preserved by generation, and transmitted to new individuals which proceed from those which have undergone these changes.

In his earlier work this was first expressed by Lamarck as follows:—

"All that Nature has caused individuals to acquire or lose by the influences of environment to which they have been long exposed, and consequently by the influence of the predominant employment of a certain organ, or by that of the continued lack of use of the same part,—all this Nature conserves by generation to the new individuals which arise, provided that these acquired variations (changements) are common to both sexes, or to those which have produced these new individuals."

This law is now known as 'the inheritance of acquired characters,' or better, to revive Lamarck's original idea expressed in the word *changements*, we should call it the theory of *inheritance of acquired changes or variations*.

This theory[1] of Lamarck is seen to be substantially similar to that of Erasmus Darwin, and to depart widely from that of Buffon, for Lamarck does not follow Buffon in supposing that environment directly produces changes in animals, either in their form or organization. In a single sentence

---

[1] *Première loi.*—La vie, par ses propres forces, tend continuellement à accroître le volume de tout corps qui la possède, et à étendre les dimensions de ses parties, jusqu'à un terme qu'elle amène elle-même.

Deuxième loi.—La production d'un nouvel organe dans un corps animal résulte d'un nouveau besoin survenu qui continue de se faire sentir, et d'un nouveau mouvement que ce besoin fait naître et entretient.

Troisième loi.—Le développement des organes et leur force d'action sont constamment en raison de l'emploi de ces organes.

Quatrième loi.—Tout ce qui a été acquis, tracé ou changé dans l'organisation des individus, pendant le cours de leur vie, est conservé par la génération et transmis aux nouveaux individus qui proviennent de ceux qui ont éprouvé ces changements.

of the *Philosophie Zoologique* he summarizes his own doctrine as follows:—

"But great changes in environment bring about changes in the habits of animals. Changes in their wants necessarily bring about parallel changes in their habits. If new wants become constant or very lasting, they form new habits, the new habits involve the use of new parts, or a different use of old parts, which results finally in the production of new organs and the modification of old ones."

Again, he says:—

"Circumstances influence the forms of animals. But I must not be taken literally, for environment can effect no direct changes whatever upon the organization of animals."

He illustrates his theory in advancing proofs that it is not the organ which gives origin to the habit, but the habit which gives origin to the organ, and points out examples of the effects of use and disuse. He refers all rudimentary structures to disuse, such as the embryonic teeth of the whalebone whales, which had recently been discovered by St. Hilaire, the eyes of the mole, and of the *Proteus*, the blind salamander of the Austrian caves. He is inconsistent with his own theory when he says that the organ of hearing has been developed everywhere by the direct action of vibrations of sound. Again, he explains the development of the webbed feet of birds, by their being attracted to swampy ground by hunger, making efforts to swim, spreading the toes, the skin being thus stretched between them.

His conception of the initial causal relation of the desires and wants of animals is illustrated in the following paragraphs:—

"I conceive that a Gasteropod mollusc, which, as it crawls along, finds the need of touching the bodies in front of it, makes efforts to touch those bodies with some of the foremost parts of the head, and sends to these every time quantities of nervous fluids as well as of other liquids; I conceive and say, that it must result from this reiterated afflux towards the point in question, that the nerves which abut at these points will, by slow degrees, be extended. Now, as in the same circumstances, other fluids of the same animal flow also to the same places, and especially nourishing fluids, it must follow that two or more tentacles will appear and develop insensibly on the points referred to."

As illustrating the sensitiveness of lowly organized animals to the action of evironment, he cites a series of his observations upon *Hydra*, when moving about in search of light.

Numerous other examples are given of the supposed origin of other parts of the body, among which we may select his account of the origin of the hoofs in mammals:

"All mammals sprang from saurians, more or less similar to our crocodiles. They first appeared under the form of amphibian mammals with four feebly developed limbs. These primitive forms divided in the manner according to which they fed. Some, accustoming themselves to browse upon shrubs, became the source of the ungulates. Advancing upon the earth, they experienced the need of having longer limbs, their toes became elongated, and the habit of resting upon their four feet during the greater part of the day has caused a thick horn to arise, which envelops the extremity of the toes of their feet. The other mammals remained amphibious, like the seals."

He also explains the origin of the horns in the ruminant animals by the efforts which they have made to butt their heads together in their periods of anger; thus has been formed a secretion of matter upon the forehead. The fleet types of ruminants which have been exposed to the attacks of carnivorous animals, have been obliged to fly, and have thus acquired the habit of making very rapid movements; thus have been formed the types of Gazelle, Deer, and so forth. Such crude illustrations certainly could not predispose his contemporaries in favour of his theory.

He was still less happy in his account of the limbs of snakes:

"The snakes sprang from reptiles with four extremities, but having taken up the habit of moving along the earth and concealing themselves among bushes, their bodies, owing to repeated efforts to elongate themselves and to pass through narrow spaces, have acquired a considerable length out of all proportion to their width. Since long feet would have been very useless, and short feet would have been incapable of moving their bodies, there resulted a cessation of use of these parts, which has finally caused them to totally disappear, although they were originally part of the plan of organization in these animals."

It is evident that Lamarck was forced to give such illustrations as these, because, shut off as he was from experiment and further observation, they were the only ones which came within his range of imagination; with all their absurdities, they present a semblance to the expressions of some modern writers.

In his theory of Heredity, Lamarck postulated the inheritance of acquired characters, which we have learned to-day is the crucial point in his whole system. He did not expand Buffon's theories in regard to the physical basis of Transmission. He brings out the results which spring from free intercrossing, showing that according to his theory, in the union of individuals which have been subjected to different environments, the effects of environment would be neutralized, whereas the crossing of individuals which had been subjected to the same environment would hasten and perpetuate the transmission of similar effects. To this principle he refers the fact that the accidental changes induced by the habits of men are not perpetuated, since they do not occur in both parents, whereas the formation of distinct races in widely different parts of the world, is due to the uniformity of their environment.

Lamarck foresaw the great difficulties which would arise in classification from his theory of the filiation and mutability of all animal and plant types, and he fully grasped the immediate bearings of the theory upon the definition of species. He writes: "Nature exhibits to us individuals succeeding each other, but the species among them have only a relative stability, and are only temporarily invariable." Quatrefages remarks that he does not clearly distinguish between species, races, and varieties.

The definition of species was in Lamarck's time the test of the creed of the naturalist. Isidore St. Hilaire, in the *Histoire Naturelle Générale*, gives us an interesting outline of the history of these definitions, beginning with that of Linnæus, including Buffon's earlier and later definitions, and Cuvier's later definitions; Lamarck's is admirable:—

"A species is a collection of similar individuals which are perpetuated by generation in the same condition, as long as their environment has not changed sufficiently to bring about variation in their habits, their character, and their form."

Certainly no better definition of a species could be given to-day.

We have seen that Lamarck's final conception of filiation, or the idea of the branching of life, had not been reached in 1802, in which he gives a vertical scale of the succession of groups of animals quite similar to that which had been developing on the false conception of phylogeny from the time of Aristotle. It is interesting, therefore, to place, side by side, his first scale of 1802 with that which he published in the *Philosophie Zoologique*, of 1809.

TABLEAU DU RÈGNE ANIMAL (1802).

Montrant la Dégradation Progressive des Organes Spéciaux jusqu'à leur Anéantissement.

Nota. — La progression de la dégradation n'est nulle part régulière ou proportionnelle; mais elle existe dans l'ensemble d'une manière évidente.

1. Les Mammaux	
2. Les Oiseaux	Une colonne vertébrale, faisant la base d'un squelette articulé.
3. Les Reptiles	
4. Les Poissons	
5. Les Mollusques	
6. Les Annelides	
7. Les Crustacés	
8. Les Arachnides	Point de colonne vertébrale; point de véritable squelette.
9. Les Insectes	
10. Les Vers	
11. Les Radiaires	
12. Les Polypes	

In 1802 he expressly speaks of the shaded gradation in the complication of organization, not as a lineal series of species, or even of genera, for he says such a series does not exist. But, " I speak of a series quite regularly gradated in its principal masses; that is to say, in the principal known systems of organization. Such a series in this case certainly offers lateral ramifications in many directions, the extremities of which are truly isolated points." This early conception of Lamarck's may be compared to a fir-tree with a single central stem and radiating branches. He says, "that such a natural series has recently been denied, and that some have substituted for a gradated series a reticulated series, in which animals and plants are spread out as upon a map. Such a reticulated series has seemed sublime to some modern writers, and Hermann has attempted to add probability to it. But those who study more profoundly the organization of living bodies, and occupy themselves less exclusively with the consideration of species, will see that this view will have to be entirely abandoned."

TABLEAU DU RÈGNE ANIMAL (1809).

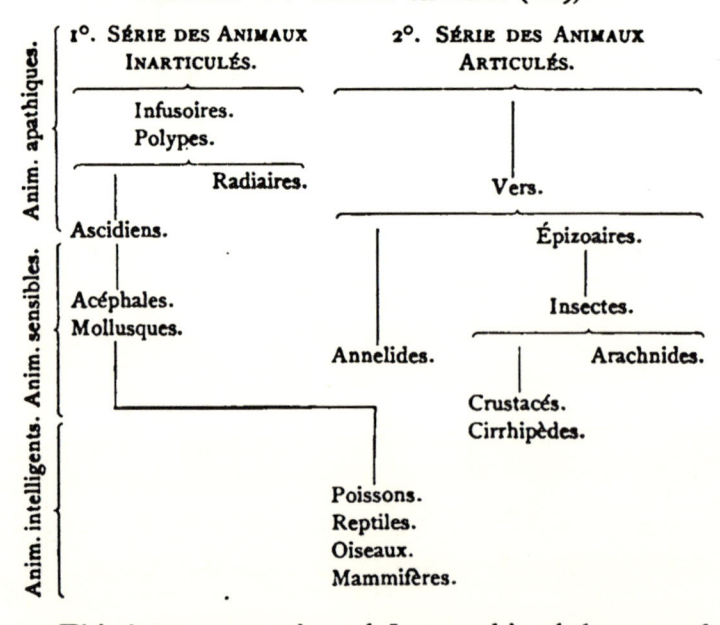

	1°. Série des Animaux Inarticulés.	2°. Série des Animaux Articulés.
Anim. apathiques.	Infusoires. Polypes.	
	Radiaires.	Vers.
Anim. sensibles.	Ascidiens.	Épizoaires.
	Acéphales. Mollusques.	Insectes.
		Arachnides.
	Annelides.	
		Crustacés. Cirrhipèdes.
Anim. intelligents.		Poissons. Reptiles. Oiseaux. Mammifères.

This later conception of Lamarck's of the tree of life as branching, not as radiating from a single central stem, but as branching from the roots into larger and smaller stems, was first published in 1809. This, so far as we know, was the first of the great phyletic trees, the construction of which has since occupied so large a portion of the energy of zoölogists, and has been carried to the farthest extreme by Haeckel.

In his second table Lamarck derives the fishes from the molluscs; but in a third table, published in 1815, while it is of the same branching character, he declares that he can no longer connect the vertebrates at any point with the invertebrates! He therefore places them by themselves, without attempting to filiate them. The third table, therefore, represents Lamarck's latest views.

His true conception of Phylogeny grew out of his appreciation of the fact that many forms of life had become extinct. He says (*Philosophie Zoologique*, Chapter 3)—"Those who have carefully examined large collections of species, are aware how they shade into each other, and that when we find species which are apparently isolated, it is only because we have not yet obtained the intermediate forms. . . . I do not wish to say that existing animals form a simple and evenly graded series, but they form a branching series, irregularly gradated, the gaps having been filled by lost forms. It follows that the species which terminate each branch of the series are related, upon one side at least, with others which shade into them." As early as 1802 he held that affinities indicate community of parentage, and that it is necessary to prove that the series which constitutes the animal scale resides essentially in the distribution of the principal masses which compose it, and not in that of the species, nor even of the genera. As we see in the above tables, Lamarck's attempts at reconstructing the tree of life were crude, but considering the infancy of Paleontology and the entire absence of embryological knowledge, his speculations appear more to his credit. He supposed that mammals passed through amphibious mammals back to saurians similar to crocodiles. The seals or aquatic mammalia gave rise to the Unguiculates or clawed animals, and when the claws became too long, the Carnivores made efforts to retract them. Some primitive mammals did not leave the water at all, but lost their limbs and became the Cetacea.

It is strange that Lamarck grasped the true idea of extinction of the lower types, but not of the higher types. He could not credit the extinction of such perfect forms as the Mastodon or the Paleotherium by any of the forces of Nature, but believed that they had probably been exterminated by man, or that these species might still be found alive elsewhere. He thoroughly believed in the extinction of lower types, for example, of the Molluscs, and that the lower types had given way to the higher, the ranks of the lower types being constantly replenished by incessant creation of the lowest forms.

As animals progressed, new forms were constantly arising in the primitive scale. One of the strongest objections which Lamarck had to meet, one which shows that his theory of Transmutation excited a lively discussion at the time, as Darwinism did afterwards, was the persistency of certain lower types. When Geoffroy St. Hilaire brought back his rich collections of mummied cats and other animals from the tombs of Egypt, and it was found that these were identical with the actual living representatives of the same species, and that these species had existed without variation between two and three thousand years, it was considered very strong evidence against the Transmutation theory. Lamarck replied that in Egypt there had been substantially no change of environment, both the soil and the climate had remained the same during that great period; that being the case, no new habits had been imposed upon animals, and the persistence of their characters was therefore readily explained.

It is also noteworthy that Lamarck, adopting for animals the indirect action of environment, adopted for plants a theory of the direct action of environment, in the absence of any nervous system whereby these organisms could respond to external stimuli. He thus coincided with Buffon in regard to plant evolution. He cites numerous instances of rapid modification by drought, by change of habitat, by cultivation, and concludes: " All is effected by changes undergone in the nutrition of the plant, in its methods of absorption, and in its transpirations, in the quantity of caloric, light, air, and humidity; finally, in the superiority which certain of its vital movements can take on over others." In his transfer from the study of Botany to Zoölogy, Lamarck's interests seem to have been wholly weaned from the study of plants. He does not show the least glimmering of the ideas of the struggle for existence among the plants, and does not by any means enlarge Buffon's ideas upon this subject.

In his speculations upon the origin of life, Lamarck at first seems to have rejected the doctrine of Abiogenesis, but later (1802) he placed the origin and continuous generation of the lowest forms of life out of inorganic matter, at the base of his scale of Evolution. He says: —

"In the waters of the ancient world, and at the present time, very small masses of mucilaginous matter were collected. Under the influences of light, certain elements, caloric and electric, entered these little bodies. These corpuscles became capable of taking in and exhaling gases; vital movements began, and thus an elemental plant or animal sprang into existence. Possibly higher forms of life, such as infest the intestines, originate in this way. Nature is thus always creating."

He believed that by these little masses of gelatinous matter, brought together by attraction, a tissue '*cellulaire*' was formed, containing gases and vital movements; that these little forms of life were the original inhabitants of the globe; moreover, that spontaneous generation of these organisms was still going on.[1]

After studying Lamarck and finding how much there is of great value in his system, we have to record that he exerted astonishingly little influence, and, in France at least, was only followed by a single writer. This was partly due to the stigma which was placed upon the transmutation theory, and the strong opposition to Lamarck's doctrine by Cuvier, the most influential naturalist of the time. As Lamarck retired from active life after the loss of his eyesight, he became a less and less known figure; he could take no direct part in spreading his doctrines, and left the arena of discussion open to Cuvier and St. Hilaire.

Lamarck, as a naturalist, exhibited exceptional powers of definition and description, while in his philosophical writings upon Evolution, his speculation far outran his observations, and his theory suffered from the absurd illustrations which he brought forward in support of it. It was such examples as the method of evolution of the snakes, which gave Lamarck's critics their opportunity of throwing all his ideas into ridicule; and from some of these brief illustrations his critics spread the impression that he believed animals acquired new organs simply by wishing for them. His really sound speculation in Zoölogy was also injured by his earlier and thoroughly worthless speculation in Chem-

[1] Oken's similar theory was not advanced until 1805.

istry and other branches of science. Another marked defect was, that Lamarck was completely carried away with the belief that his theory of the transmission of acquired characters was adequate to explain all the phenomena. He did not, like his contemporaries, Erasmus Darwin and Goethe, perceive and point out, that certain problems in the origin of adaptations were still left wholly untouched and unsolved. Believing that he saw a great Evolution factor, and applying it to organic nature, he was blind to its deficiencies and to every other factor, and sought to establish it as a sufficient explanation of every change in the animal world. His arguments are, in most cases, not inductive, but deductive, and are frequently found not to support his law, but to postulate it. Another defect was his limited conception of Natural Environment, in which he was inferior to his contemporary, Treviranus. Treviranus and St. Hilaire enlarged upon Buffon's view of Environment, while Lamarck did not. The greatest gap in his reasoning has become obvious since his time; namely, that it turned upon the assumption that acquired characters are inherited; this he took for granted and never endeavoured to demonstrate.

None the less we must close by placing Lamarck in the first rank. He was the first naturalist to become profoundly convinced of the great law, and to place it in the form of a system; he suffered social and scientific ostracism for this conviction, maintaining and repeating his arguments to his death-bed. There is a pathetic strain in the introduction to the last edition of his *Animaux sans Vertèbres*:—

"Avant d'atteindre le terme de mon existence, j'ai pensé que dans un nouvel ouvrage, susceptible d'être considéré comme une seconde édition de mon *Système des Animaux sans Vertèbres*, je devais exposer les principaux faits que j'ai recueillis pour mes leçons. . . . Ainsi que mes observations et mes réflexions sur la source de ces faits."

JOHANN WOLFGANG GOETHE (1749-1832) was the greatest poet of Evolution; he saw the law as a poet, as a philosopher, and as an anatomist.

While making the most substantial contributions to the scientific evidences, he did not, like his French contemporary, formulate a system. He was born five years later and died three years earlier than Lamarck, yet never knew of his writings. This circumstance Haeckel truly calls a tragic loss to science, for Goethe would have made the buried *Philosophie Zoologique* known to the world.

The brilliant early achievements of Goethe in science afford another illustration of the union of imagination and powers of observation as the essential characteristics of the naturalist. When he took his journey into Italy, and the poetic instinct began to predominate over the scientific, science lost a disciple who would have ranked among the very highest, if not the highest. Of this time Goethe says: "I have abandoned my master Loder for my friend Schiller, and Linnæus for Shakespeare." Yet Goethe, in the midst of poetry, never lost his passion for scientific studies. He seems to have felt instinctively that what contemporary science needed was not only observation, but generalization. He showed his own power of scientific generalization in his famous studies upon the metamorphoses of plants, and in his discovery (later independently reached by Oken) of the vertebrate theory of the skull, which, indeed, was only a part of his contribution to Comparative Osteology and Anatomy.

His inspiration was undoubtedly drawn partly from Buffon and largely from the school of German natural philosophers. He also imbibed the Greek influence, and in his general view of Nature, expressed in his *Gott und Welt*, we see the ideas of God working in Nature and of the unity of the development process. This he also brought out in the dialogue between Thales and Anaxagoras in the *Walpurgisnacht*. Here is unfolded the conception of the uniformity of past and present processes in Geology and Cosmogony. It is astonishing that Goethe never came across the works of Lamarck. He anticipated Lamarck as an evolutionist in his *Metamorphoses of Plants*, which was published in 1790, and the Lamarckian principle is one in which he would have undoubtedly felt the deepest interest. His sympathies in France were wholly with Geoffroy St. Hilaire and his contention for Philosophical Anatomy and Philosophical Biology. Showing that to the very last Goethe took the keenest interest in science, and placed the movements of scientific thought above political revolutions, we learn of his following the debates between St. Hilaire and Cuvier; here is the famous incident of his eighty-first year, told by Soret, and quoted by Haeckel:—

"Monday, Aug. 2d, 1830.— The news of the outbreak of the revolution of July arrived in Weimar to-day, and has caused general excitement. In the course of the afternoon I went to Goethe. 'Well,' he exclaimed as I entered, 'what do you think of this great event? The volcano has burst forth, all is in flames, and there are no more negotiations behind closed doors.' 'A dreadful affair,' I answered; 'but what else could be expected under the circumstances, and with such a ministry, except that it would end in the expulsion of the present royal family?' 'We do not seem to understand each other, my dear friend,' replied Goethe. 'I am not speaking of those people at all; I am interested in something very different. I mean the dispute between Cuvier and Geoffroy de Saint Hilaire, which has broken out in the Academy, and which is of such great importance to science.' This remark of Goethe's came upon me so unexpectedly that I did not know what to say, and my thoughts for some minutes seemed to have come to a complete standstill. 'The affair is of the utmost importance,' he continued, 'and you cannot form any idea of what I felt on receiving the news of the meeting on the 19th. In Geoffroy de Saint Hilaire we have now a mighty ally for a long time to come. But I see also how great the sympathy of the French scientific world must be in this affair, for, in spite of the terrible political excitement, the meeting on the 19th was attended by a full house. The best of it is, however, that the synthetic treatment of Nature, introduced into France by Geoffroy, can now no longer be stopped. This matter has now become public through the discussions in the Academy, carried on in the presence of a large audience; it can no longer be referred to secret committees, or be settled or suppressed behind closed doors.'"

It is not surprising that Goethe was appreciated in France, and that he was highly praised by Isidore St. Hilaire. In Cuvier we find the following allusion to his essays on Comparative Anatomy: "One finds in them, with astonishment, nearly all the propositions which have been separately advanced in recent times." And Richard Owen, somewhat later, wrote: "Goethe had taken the lead in his inquiries into Comparative Osteology." Carus, in his preface to his *Transcendental Anatomy*, wrote: "If we go back as far as possible into the history of the labours undertaken with the view to arrive at the philosophic conception of the skeleton, we find that the first idea of the metamorphosis of the osseous forms; that is, that all forms are but modifications, more or less traceable, of one and the same type; this idea belongs to Goethe."

The 'unity of type' hypothesis, which exercised such a potent influence in Europe, was developed in Goethe's mind in 1796; this was the conception which formed the chief basis of his idea of Evolution:—

"Thus much, then, we have gained, that we may assert, without hesitation, that all the more perfect organic natures, such as fishes, amphibious animals, birds, mammals, and man at the head of the list, were all formed upon one original type, which varies only more or less in parts which are none the less permanent, and which still daily changes and modifies its form by propagation."

With him, this unity of type was broadly based upon his own observations, and was partly a generalization. This led him to a correct explanation of half-developed, or vestigial, structures, which are among the strongest evidences of the law of Evolution. He thoroughly understood the relations of the anatomy of man to that of lower forms, and speaks of vestigial structures in man as follows: "These structures, which in lower organisms are developed in stronger measure, and in man, in spite of his higher organism, are not wholly lost." It was this interpretation as a working hypothesis, which led to one of Goethe's most brilliant achievements in Comparative Anatomy,— his prediction of the discovery of premaxillary bones in man. This raised a storm of opposition which now seems hardly credible, in spite of which Goethe succeeded in verifying his prediction.

Thus, Goethe stepped from observation to generalization, from generalization to the working hypothesis, which he turned into use as the guide to fresh research. He advanced upon the truly modern scientific method; yet, he always preserved the proper balance between observation and generalization. He says of Kant, that, if he had once held Kant's conception of derivation and of filiation, as deduced by reason, and could have undertaken lines of inquiry, nothing would have prevented him from carrying out its proofs.

He was superior to all his three contemporaries, Lamarck, Treviranus, and St. Hilaire, in his realization that certain problems were very far from solution; in a work, written in 1794-95, but not published until long afterwards, he remarked that, "the question for future naturalists will be to determine how, for instance, cattle got their horns, and not for what they are used." He thus, with Kant, felt the gap in the lack of a natural explanation for the origin of purposive structures.

Goethe's theory of the factors, so far as formulated, had the spirit of Buffon and Lamarck, and is beautifully expressed in the passage Haeckel selects from his *Metamorphosis of Animals* (1819):—

"All members develop themselves according to eternal laws,
And the rarest form mysteriously preserves the primitive type.
Form, therefore, determines the animal's way of life,
And in turn the way of life powerfully reacts upon all form.
Thus the orderly growth of form is seen to hold
Whilst yielding to change from externally acting causes."[1]

In his *Metamorphoses of Plants*, published in 1790, we find Goethe's ideas clearly expressed. He here derives all plants from a single original form, and all the elaborate structures of the plant from the leaf. He called his theory, '*Bildung und Umbildung*,' or 'Formation and Transformation.'

[1] This contains the Aristotelian 'matter and form' notion, together with a perception of the factors of Lamarck (4th line) and of Buffon (6th line).

The 'Urbild,' or type, was composed of the internal original common characters, or, as we should say, the 'stem characters,' lying at the base of all forms, and these original structures were preserved by heredity.

The preservation of this type was opposed by a continuous progressive development, and this was necessitated by the relations of the organism to the outer world. The former, or type, is the centripetal structural force, or specification; while the latter, or progressive development, is the centrifugal structural force, or metamorphosis. Goethe prized highly the conception of these two opposed forces, which we now know as Heredity and Variation, or Inheritance and Adaptation. Morphology was Goethe's favourite study, and upon transformation depended all his ideas of the Descent theory. Phyletic series, and the methods of ascertaining them, were wholly unknown to him, but structural series, or the modifications of a primitive type or archetype, exhibited successively in the lower and higher types of plants and in the lower and higher types of animals, were clearly perceived, and, as we have seen above, they led Goethe to a thoroughly philosophical interpretation of structures in all stages of Evolution, in the three phases of Development, Balance, and Degeneration.

GOTTFRIED REINHOLD TREVIRANUS (1776–1837), a prominent German naturalist and contemporary of Lamarck and Goethe, has the distinction of defining 'Biology' as the science of living Nature, in 1802. It is an interesting coincidence that both he and Lamarck independently felt the need of a comprehensive term for the principles underlying Botany and Zoölogy, and proposed it in the same year.

Huxley has also placed Treviranus beside Lamarck as one of the founders of the Evolution theory; but a careful study of Treviranus' chief work — *Biologie oder Philosophie der lebenden Natur* — does not justify our ranking these two men together. In the other extreme, Treviranus, as an evolutionist, has been too widely ignored. He is not named by any of the French writers; his own countryman, Haeckel, has shown his position clearly, but places him below Oken. I may give a rather full statement of his views. His *Biologie* was published several years after Lamarck's first essay upon Evolution, but in the preface of his last work, — *Erscheinungen und Gesetze des Organischen Lebens*, which was published in 1830, — Treviranus states that he had reached his conclusions independently of and prior to Lamarck. Even in this case we cannot claim for Treviranus great originality; for in his conception of Evolution he does not advance very far beyond the standpoint reached by Buffon in his middle period, and he appears to us rather as a very careful student and compiler not only of Buffon but of Leibnitz, Kant, Schelling, — all of whom suggested the

Evolution theory,—also of Linnæus, Harvey, and Blumenbach. He had moreover the advantage of the new Paleontology of Cuvier and of the travels of Humboldt.

His point of approach to Nature is that of the German natural philosophers. He places life upon the chemical and mechanical basis, and in his introduction enters a vigorous protest against the purely speculative work upon the one side,—*die Träume und Visionen*,—probably having in mind his worthy predecessor Bonnet and others whom I have placed in the speculative group. On the other side, he protests against the dry systematic work which Linnæus had left to his posterity,— his terms without his genius,—a Botany and Zoölogy devoid of all higher generalizations.

"An author," he says, "can have no sadder and more spirit-killing duty than the reading and writing of compilations. The teachings of Natural Science have long been standing isolated like the pyramids in the deserts of Egypt, as if the value of Natural History were not rather the application than the mere possession of facts. What have Botany and Zoölogy been hitherto, but a dry register of names, and what man who has not lost his sense for higher work can find time for these gymnastics of memory? But once regard systematic work as a part of Biology, and nomenclature as a means rather than as an end, and both take their place in science, contributing to the whole in which the intellect of man perceives the unity and harmony of Natural Law. Even the work of Linnæus, as it does not reach the highest point, is mere construction. The author will give opinion and theory a place in this work, but he is far from those who give their dreams and fancies a reality and permanence, believing that his own theories may perish, and hoping to direct the current of thought in Biology to adapt itself to Nature, and not to make Nature adapt herself to the current of thought. Let us not direct the stream of Nature, but be directed by her. Let us publish a work which will collect the numerous thoughts lying scattered throughout the writings of Natural History, and this generalization will have greater value than all the descriptions of new forms."

Treviranus thus ranges himself with the school of Buffon, Lamarck, Geoffroy St. Hilaire, and Goethe, as against the school of Linnæus and Cuvier. He believed that it was possible to discover the Philosophy of Nature, and his whole work is written in an admirable spirit. In the succeeding introductory chapters upon the interpretation of living Nature, he considers the importance of Biology, its fundamental principles, possible systems of Biology, methods of experimental Biology, as well as the use of the hypothesis, — that is, the working hypothesis, — as the essential weapon of progress towards the truth. He defines Biology as "the study of the different forms and appearances of organic life, of the conditions and laws under which these exist, and of the causes by which they are kept in operation." In the *Laws of Life* (p. 58), he points out that every part of the organism is subservient to the whole, that Nature never builds up one organ or system of organs without causing others to suffer reduction. This is equivalent to the '*loi de balancement*' of St. Hilaire, or the modern law of 'compensation of growth,' the deficiency of one part being made up by the greater development of another. He also, as clearly as Lamarck, perceives the causal relation between function and structure. In his conception of natural environment, he with Schelling perceives that every class of animals exerts upon living Nature influences similar to those exerted in the animal or plant by their organs and systems of organs upon each other.

He has two chief thoughts in regard to environment. First, the influences of life upon life, and of life upon Nature; and second, the constant revolutions of life and climate. He says that the wider the limits reached by the action or by the incidence or impact of environment upon the living organism, so much higher the grade of the organism must be. The lowest rudiments of life — *vita minima* — are those in which the action of environment falls with least specialization, and these rudiments mark the transition to lifeless matter. This conception of environment, as the action and reaction of life upon Nature and of life upon life, he amplifies in connection with the law of Buffon and Malthus, that the struggle for existence consists, not only in reproduction, but in reproduction increasing in quantity according to the destructive influences of surrounding life. An animal must have more progeny as the number of its enemies increases.

We thus see that Treviranus breathed the spirit of the most philosophical of his predecessors, and was essentially modern in his method. We, therefore, expect to find an equal breadth of view in his treatment of the problem of Evolution. Here we are disappointed, for we find only another proof of the insuperable difficulties under which these early evolutionists laboured, in the comparatively limited knowledge they possessed of the forms and successions of life. As soon as Treviranus departs from these first principles of Biology and undertakes an application of these principles to a theory of development of animal life, he becomes more and more speculative, and shows himself much inferior to Lamarck in his approach to the truth.

In his conception of Evolution, we see him translating Buffon's term '*dénaturée,*' by 'degeneration'; for he means by 'degeneration' exactly what we now term 'adaptation,' or modification, by the action of external formative forces; in other words, both development and degeneration. His theory of the Evolution factors is very similar to that of Buffon, as he traces degeneration solely to the influences of varying external conditions, and this he believes to be the modifying factor in single organisms. The perpetual changes in living surroundings bring about constant changes in the organization of the body.

In course of these changes old species are destroyed and new ones take their places. He brings out clearly the idea of the action of environment in the elimination of species, groups, and families, but does not assign this as a cause of the origin of adaptations. Thus, many species become extinct, while others become diminished in numbers. Man, himself, exhibits the direct modifying influence of his environment by wide variations in his structure. The history of the older geological periods is given us in the succession of fossils. Here, Treviranus added to the work of Cuvier the idea of modification in time, an idea which Cuvier never adopted.

Continuing to extend his Evolution theory (Vol. III., p. 225), we find that he believed in Abiogenesis: —

Every form of life can be produced by physical forces in one of two ways: either by coming into being out of formless (inorganic) matter, or by the modification of an already existing form by a continued process of shaping. . . . Wherever Nature has exerted her building forces she has brought forth Autochthones, living bodies,

*. . . qui rupto robore nati,
Compositive luto, nullos habuere parentes.*

Wherever like conditions prevailed, of climate, earth, water, atmosphere, and a similar geographical position, these Autochthones were similar, and the species which developed from them remained similar as long as the environment was unaltered. But in studying the form of any particular country, it is very hard to determine which forms are native or autochthonous, and which have spread into the country by migration from other countries.

He then proceeds to anachronistic theories of the abiogenetic origin of these Autochthones: —

"But how did these species arise? Were they born fully formed, like Aphrodite, from sea-foam? Or as simple zoöphytes? They could only have arisen by the development from generation to generation of similar forms; these primitive forms are the Encrinites, Pentacrinites, Ammonites, and other zoöphytes of the Old World, from which all organisms of the higher classes have arisen. Each species has its period of growth, of full bloom, and decline; the latter is a period of degeneration. Thus, it is not only the great catastrophes of Nature which have caused extinction, but the completion of cycles of existence, out of which new cycles have begun. Thus, in Nature, all is in a state of flux and transfer; even man has not reached the highest term of his existence, but will progress to still higher regions, and produce a nobler type of being."

These sentences show that Treviranus did not add anything to the main theory of Evolution, although a strong advocate of it. His ideas upon descent are much less clear and accurate than those of Lamarck; and in his views of the original, spontaneous origin of some of the higher forms of life, as shown in the sentence last quoted, he is very far afield. Haeckel is mistaken when he states that Treviranus refers to the lowest organisms in the term 'zoöphytes,' for Treviranus couples with this term such complex forms as Crinoids and Ammonites. As to the factors of Evolution, he does not advance beyond Buffon, and in his general conception he virtually takes the position held much earlier by Goethe, for he summarizes his views in the sentence: "In every living being there exists the capability of an endless variety of form-assumption; each possesses the power to adapt its organization to the changes of the outer world, and it is this power, put into action by the change of the universe, that has raised the simple zoöphytes of the primitive world to continually higher stages of organization, and has introduced a countless variety of species into animate Nature."

GEORGES CUVIER (1769–1832), as the great opponent of Lamarckian doctrines in particular, of Evolution in general, and of the methods of thought which were surely leading to its demonstration, deserves a few words in this history. It is interesting to note that in forming his personal opinions, he reversed the order taken by Linnæus, Lamarck, and St. Hilaire; for, starting with views very similar to the most advanced held by Buffon upon the mutability of species, he arrived at a point as conservative as the early position of Linnæus, insisting upon the fixity, not only of species, but of varieties. His definition was of the kind destined to prevail until 1858. "All the beings belonging to one of these forms (perpetuated since the beginning of all things, that is, the Creation) constitute what we call species." As head of the illustrious *École des Faits*, he laughed, and set his pupils laughing, over the 'Philosophy of Nature,' characterizing it as '*La fête de la fête.*'

It is strange that whenever Cuvier left his objective studies for speculation, he was exceptionally unsound; in his Embryology he believed in 'Evolution' *versus* 'Epigenesis'; in his *Discours sur les Révolutions sur la Surface du Globe*, he advocated the doctrine of Catastrophism *versus* Uniformity; he also advanced, and later retracted, the theory of a 'succession of special creations.' As the chief founder of Comparative Anatomy and Paleontology, he introduced the modern conception of Paleontology as past Zoölogy. He first described *Anchitherium*, and pointed out its resemblance to the Horse; this is a form which, perhaps, more than any other, is to-day part of the most convincing fossil testimony of Evolution; yet Cuvier failed to see in it any proofs of the 'filiation' hypothesis he was opposing. His influence was almost unbounded; a favourite of Napoleon, he was able to build up a great school in the Jardin des Plantes, and exerted his political influence in keeping the 'transformists' out of position. He was followed by De Candolle, the botanist, by Duméril, the invertebrate zoölogist, by De Blainville, the paleontologist; in Germany, by Vogt and Bronn. Richard Owen partly shared Cuvier's views, and partly those of St. Hilaire.

GEOFFROY ST. HILAIRE (1772–1844), another of the distinguished French naturalists of the early part of this century, was long a colleague of Lamarck in the Jardin des Plantes. We cannot read his works without perceiving that he was by birth a philosopher, and by adoption a naturalist. Although his theory of the causes was profoundly different from that of Lamarck, he belonged to the Buffon-Lamarck school of thought, as opposed to

that of Cuvier, and in support of this school his
name came into wide celebrity by the famous discussion of 1830 in the French Academy of Sciences,
to which Goethe alluded. He added largely to
the evidences of 'filiation' and contributed several entirely original theoretical 'factors' of transformation; nevertheless, there is an undercurrent
of doubt as to the extent of the law of Evolution,
in all his writings. He was not a radical evolutionist like Lamarck.

Perrier, Quatrefages, and the younger St. Hilaire
have carefully studied his opinions and history.
St. Hilaire was a pupil of Buffon, but as a thinker
he mainly acknowledges his debt to the German
Natural Philosophers and especially to Schelling
in his researches upon the philosophy of Nature;
although he does not follow Schelling in his advocacy of the superiority of the deductive method.

St. Hilaire's method was professedly inductive.
Ideas, he said, should be directly engendered by
facts. His conceptions were often *a priori*, but his
demonstrations were always *a posteriori*. In his
speculation upon Evolution, we see that St. Hilaire
was by no means always consistent with his method,
but was very largely influenced by certain classes
of facts which came under his direct observation,
and reasoned from these to laws touching facts of
quite a distinct character. Goethe says of him:
"He recalls Buffon in some points of view. He
does not stop at Nature existing or achieved; he

studies it in the germ, in its development, and in its future. He projects the idea of unity, which Buffon had just touched upon." There were three branches of study in which St. Hilaire was most deeply interested. First, Comparative Anatomy; second, Teratology; and third, what came to be known as Philosophical Anatomy when he finally embodied it in the *Philosophie Anatomique*. This was published in 1818, and was the work so greatly admired by Goethe. The narrower range of his studies, the dominating influence of his 'unity of type' principle and the sudden departures from type seen in his pathological studies, shaped the growth of St. Hilaire's limited and peculiar view of Evolution.

He has been mistakenly spoken of as the successor of Lamarck. It is simply true that he took up the general doctrines of transformism at the point where Lamarck could no longer defend them. As a remarkable coincidence, Buffon, Lamarck, and Hilaire all became transformists at the same age of life. His son, Isidore St. Hilaire, as well as Quatrefages and Perrier, show very clearly that he was more properly the disciple and expander of Buffon. He denied the inherited influences of habit, which formed Lamarck's central thought, and maintained that the direct action of environment was the sole cause of transformation, always regarding organisms as comparatively passive in their '*milieu*.' Thus he found it necessary to greatly differentiate Buffon's conception of environment, especially on its chemical atmospheric side, attributing very marked results to its influence upon the respiratory functions, as in his account of the evolution of the crocodiles from the saurians.

It was between 1825 and 1828 that Geoffroy published his memoirs upon the fossil Teleosaurs of Caen, and connected them by theoretical descent with the existing Gavials.[1] Changing environment and respiration were, he believed, the chief factors in this transformation.[2]

"Le monde ambiant est tout puissant pour une altération des corps organisés. . . . La respiration constitue, selon moi, une ordonnée si puissante pour la disposition des formes animales qu'il n'est même point nécessaire que le milieu des fluides respiratoire se modifie brusquement et fortement, pour occasioner des formes très peu sensiblement altérées."

The atmosphere, acting upon the pulmonary cells, brings about "*modifications which are favourable or destructive ('funestes'); these are inherited, and they influence all the rest of the organization of the animal because if these modifications lead to injurious effects, the animals which exhibit them perish and are replaced by others of a somewhat different form, a form changed so as to be adapted to (à la convenance) the new environment.*" This is a very striking statement of a law of variation due to the influences of environment, and of the survival or extinction of

[1] *Recherches sur des grands Sauriens trouvés à l'état fossile.* Mém. Acad. d. Sciences, Paris, 1831.
[2] *Influence du monde ambiant pour modifier les formes animales.* Mém. de l'Acad. d. Sc., XII., p. 63, 1833.

types according to the favourable or unfavourable character of the variation. Perrier italicizes this passage and points out its anticipation of Darwinism.

Another highly characteristic feature of his theory was, that he included in it what has recently been termed '*saltatory evolution*,' and strongly opposed Lamarck's fundamental principle that all transformation is extremely slow. It is evident that this idea was suggested to him by the sudden transformations observed in his teratological studies. This enabled him to maintain Evolution without demonstrating the existence of intermediate forms. Intermediate forms had begun to be a stumbling-block to evolutionists. Where, it was asked, was evidence of a transition between amphibians and reptiles, and between reptiles and birds? This also enabled St. Hilaire to avoid a difficulty he himself raised, that characters of new forms of life would not be maintained pure, owing to the blends of interbreeding; these sudden saltations or leaps from type to type secured the necessary physiological isolation. As a rapid transformationist, he was not, however, an imitator of De Maillet, who, we remember, believed in the transformation of adult forms. St. Hilaire denied the possibility of these rapid leaps in the adult condition, and believed that they took place mainly in the embryonic condition; here, the underlying causes of sudden transformation were profound changes induced in the egg by external influences, accidents as it were, regulated by law.

As it involved rapid, as well as gradual, transformation, St. Hilaire's system did not always require the existence of intermediate links. For instance, he advanced as an hypothesis the suggestion that the first bird might have issued directly from the egg laid by a reptile, and, as a bird could not be fertilized or intercrossed by its reptilian relatives, the new characters could not be suppressed by intercrossing: "It is evidently not by an insensible change that the inferior types of oviparous vertebrates have given rise to the superior organization of the group of birds. An accident, within the range of possibility, and not very great in its original production, but of an incalculable importance in all its effects, has sufficed to produce in all parts of the body the conditions of the bird type."

Finally, his attitude towards transformism, as explaining all forms of life, was much less positive and sweeping than Lamarck's. His view of Evolution may be summed up in this sentence: "Species vary with their environment, and existing species have descended by modification from earlier and somewhat simpler species." He admitted that the question to be decided by future paleontological research, is whether "the living forms of to-day have descended by a succession of generations, and without break, from the extinct forms of the antediluvian period." He looked for, and found, proofs and evidences, within his own reach, in Embryology, in the history of metamorphoses and in Teratology.

Not even in speculation did he trace back all forms of life to a simple prototype; he thus narrowed Lamarck's wide field of conjecture in Phylogeny.

We find a full account of the famous discussion of the year 1830, between St. Hilaire and Cuvier, in Perrier's *Philosophie Zoologique avant Darwin*. It is also frequently alluded to in the *Histoire Naturelle Générale*, by the younger St. Hilaire.

Linnæus opened his *Systema Naturæ* with the statement that the true greatness of man consists in his observing, reasoning, and forming conclusions, but the main tendency of his own work was to carry his conclusions only to the point of distinguishing between the separate forms of life, not to the causes of these distinctions. Buffon held that the first aim of science was to describe exactly, and to determine particular facts, but that we must devote ourselves to something higher; namely, to combine and generalize upon the facts, and to judge particular causes in the light of the more general causes of Nature. Thus, Linnæus and Buffon were the founders of two distinct schools. Linnæus was upheld by Cuvier and all the systematic writers; Buffon by Lamarck, Treviranus, Goethe, and St. Hilaire. Into this higher region of generalization, which Goethe took up only to abandon, few naturalists dared to stir. The followers of Linnæus showed themselves weakest where they attempted deduction, and we have contrasted the soundness of Cuvier's Comparative Anatomy with the worthlessness of his speculation. The Buffon school came into ridicule by some of the wild hypotheses in their earlier books; for neither Buffon nor Lamarck knew when to apply the curb. Excessive speculation brought a reaction. After Kielmeyer, Schelling, and Goethe, there was a return to the older methods of simple observation and record. As we have seen, this was partly justified by the fact that the whole philosophy of the speculative writers, and much of that of Buffon and Lamarck, was deductive, rather than inductive. Geoffroy St. Hilaire sought to revive speculation and place it upon the true inductive-deductive basis in his *Philosophie Anatomique.*

On the 15th February, 1830, matters came to a crisis; St. Hilaire read before the Academy of Sciences at Paris, in the name of Latreille and himself, a report upon the investigations of two young naturalists. The conclusions reached in the report were advanced in support of St. Hilaire's chief doctrine of the *universal unity of plan of composition;* this was his central life thought, leading him to emphasize the resemblances rather than the differences between animals, and to lay the foundation of the study of 'parallelism' in development. In this case he was illustrating his principle by the supposed analogy between the organization of some cephalopod molluscs and the vertebrates. It seemed to Cuvier that these conclusions constituted a direct attack, and this brought on a discussion of the questions which had been marking a widening gap between the opinions of the two great schools. Cuvier replied by a criticism of the position of St. Hilaire as to this 'unity of plan,' and rightly sought to demonstrate that there were several distinct plans of animal organization. He carefully analyzed the arguments brought forward, and showed conclusively that in the types cited by St. Hilaire the organs in their position gave evidence simply of analogy and of resemblance, not of a real unity of plan; that these molluscs led to no other types. Further, he said that St. Hilaire's method contained nothing new, and reverted simply to the views of Aristotle.

In following the details of this discussion, we see that Cuvier was entirely correct in his facts, and wrong in his principle; while St. Hilaire was wrong in his facts, and right in the principle which he advocated. The effect was to drive Cuvier, who issued with the greater *éclat*, into the extreme position of recommending naturalists to confine themselves solely to the exposition of positive facts without attempting to draw from them inductions. This sharp issue, therefore, exerted a retarding influence upon the progress of inquiry into Evolution; for Cuvier, in his brilliant lectures in the Collége de France, threw increased weight against the method and teachings of St. Hilaire, as he had previously done against those of Lamarck.

BORY DE SAINT VINCENT (1780-1846) seems to have been the only loyal successor of Lamarck in

France. Like his leader, he was both a naturalist, and, for a time, an army officer. In the former capacity, he was, for a time, with the expedition of Baudin. Quatrefages has given the following sketch of his views:

In several papers, but especially in the article 'Creation' of the *Dictionnaire Classique de l'Histoire Naturelle*, of which he was the editor, he developed, in more than one point, the doctrines of Lamarck, and drew from them conclusions which belonged to himself.

Bory admits the spontaneous daily formation of new species, not, it is true, upon our continents, which have for a long time been peopled with both animals and plants, but only in countries considered by him less ancient in formation. He cites, for example, the island of Madagascar, which he believes to have only recently issued from the sea, under the influence of volcanic forces. According to him, this island contains more "polymorphic species than all the *terra firma* of the Old World." On this relatively modern soil he says species are not yet fixed. Nature, in hastening to constitute the types, seems to have neglected to regulate the accessory organs. On the other hand, in the continents more anciently formed, the development of plants has, perforce, followed an identical route for an incalculable number of generations. The plants have thus become arrested in their types, and do not present the variations so frequent in new countries. Bory thus introduces a new idea in the influence exercised on the fixation of specific characters by the action of a long series of ancestors placed under constant conditions. According to him, this, so to speak, is habit exercising its powers, not only on individuals, but even on species. But in this conception, without being apparently aware of it, he places himself in formal contradiction to the master of whom he proclaims himself a disciple. We have seen, in fact, that in the opinion of Lamarck, all organized forms were being constantly modified according to new needs, and it follows that each generation was separated more and more from its ancestors. While with Bory heredity would have, as its result, the fixation of characters, with Lamarck it is constantly causing them to vary, by accumulating the little differences acquired in each generation. In this point of view, Bory must be regarded as an aberrant disciple of Lamarck. The idea of Bory, of the fixation of characters by heredity, was subsequently taken up and enlarged by his countryman, Naudin.

ISIDORE ST. HILAIRE (1805–1861) serves us as a mirror of the further recession of opinion from transformism in France. The tide of hostile influence had set too strongly against the doctrine; and we find the son taking a still more conservative position than his father, whom, nevertheless, he loyally defended.

He advanced a theory of 'the *limited* variability

of species' (rather than of the mutability) in his classic work, *Histoire Générale et Particulière d'Anomalies de l'Organization*, 1832, and his *L'Histoire Naturelle des Règnes Organiques*. He was undoubtedly swayed by the difficulty of finding positive evidence for transformation, and further by the negative evidence of the stability of species afforded by the rich collections of mummied animals brought back from Egypt. Thus, in his theory, he dwelt upon the limited variability rather than the mutability of species, believing in transmission only to the point of forming a new race. This is fully set forth in his *Histoire Naturelle* (Vol. I., p. 431). At the conclusion of his review of the history of opinion upon Evolution in France, he gives it, as his own opinion, that characters are neither actually fixed nor variable, both depending upon the fixity or the variability of environment. New characters are the resultant of two forces: first, the modifying influence of new surroundings; and, second, the conserving influence of Heredity. When the former predominates, variations result, such as are seen among savages and in the domestication of animals. These variations among wild animals extend to modifications of colour and external characters, but in domestication the differences are much more marked. So much for changes going on at the present time. As to past time, the 'theory of limited variability' links itself with that of 'filiation,' or descent from analogous forms, as opposed to that of Cuvier of 'successive creations,' or of migration of existing species from other quarters of the globe. He concludes by saying, very guardedly, that this acceptance of the transmutation theory rests upon the actual very limited state of evidence.

It is another striking coincidence that in the very year (1859) in which this passage was published the *Origin of Species* appeared. The last stages of the decline of the main 'transmutation' movement in France were coincident with its sudden and final revival and establishment in England.

VI.

DARWIN.

Es ist für Menschen ungereimt, auch nur einen solchen Anschlag zu fassen, oder zu hoffen, dass noch etwa dereinst ein Newton aufstehen könne, der auch nur die Erzeugung eines Grashalms nach Naturgesetzen, die keine Absicht geordnet hat, begreiflich machen werde, sondern man muss diese Einsicht dem Menschen schlechterdings absprechen. — KANT.

WITH Bory de St. Vincent and the younger St. Hilaire the original movement in France, which had begun with Buffon and extended over nearly a hundred years, came to a close. In the meantime, from the early part of the century, the seed had been scattering. In England, on the Continent, and in America, the Evolution theory found here and there a friend who passingly restated, or slightly expanded, views already expressed by Buffon, Lamarck, Goethe, or Treviranus. Some original ideas also sprang up in out of the way quarters, and have been unearthed from their hiding-places since the theory has been established; we must place them, as it were, in an alcove of this history, because they certainly had little or no direct connection with the main development of the Evolution idea; they were not put forth as part of a general system, and exerted no influence upon either Darwin or Wallace.

The First Half-Century.

Darwin, in his *Historical Sketch of the Progress of Opinion*, and Haeckel, in his *Schöpfungsgeschichte*, have outlined the views of these miscellaneous contributors to the Evolution theory. The most surprising thought raised by a review of the original works, and of the passages quoted by the above authors, is that so many came near the theory and were neither captured by it nor drawn on to its further serious exposition as the key to the history of life. Only one writer between 1809 and 1858 came out in a really vigorous and sustained defence of the evolutionary system of the Universe. This was the unknown author of the *Vestiges of Creation*.

We are now familiar with the main sources of suggestion, and can consider some of these writers more critically than Darwin or Haeckel have done, from the standpoint of originality. It would be interesting to know whether Wells, for example, who so clearly set forth the Natural Selection theory in 1813, had seen any of the other 'anticipations' which have been quoted. So with the two other 'selectionists,' Matthew and Naudin. There were a series of original writers who independently approached Evolution upon the embryological side, such as Meckel, Von Baer, and Serres. Others advocated or independently advanced the laws suggested by Buffon, of modification due to the direct action of environment under the influence of wide geographical distribution. Among these were Herbert von Buch, Haldeman, and Schaafhausen the anthropologist. We find a partial revival of Goethe's doctrines by the botanists Schleiden and Lecoq.

Lamarckism found very few followers. The Greek idea of pre-existent germs of species was revived by Keyserling. The Aristotelian notion of an internal impulse or tendency towards progression was more or less clearly revived by the 'progressionists' in the *Vestiges of Creation* and in Owen's essay on the " Nature of Limbs."

Other writers who expressed a more or less positive belief in the mutability of species were: Virey[1] in 1817, Grant[2] in 1826, Rafinesque[3] in 1836, Dujardin[4] in 1843, d'Halloy[5] in 1846. Chevreul[6] and Godron,[7] in 1846 and 1847, advanced views somewhat similar to those of the younger St. Hilaire. We note also Leidy in 1850, T. Unger, the botanist, in 1852, Carus and Schaafhausen[8] in 1853, Lecoq in 1854.[9]

Sachs has shown how the botanists Brown, Nägeli, and Hofmeister were approaching the theory.

[1] Article " Espèces," *Dict. d'Hist. Naturelle de Déterville*.
[2] *Edinburgh Philosophical Journal*, Vol. XIV., p. 283.
[3] *New Flora of North America*, 1836, pp. 6, 18.
[4] *Ann. d. Sc. Nat.*, 3ᵉ sér., t. IV., p. 279.
[5] *Bulletins de l'Académie Roy. Bruxelles*, tom. XIII., p. 581.
[6] *Considérations Générales sur les Variations des Individus*. Mém. d. l. Soc. Roy. et Centr. d'Agriculture, 1846, p. 287.
[7] *De l'Espèce et des Races*. Mém. d. l. Société d. Sciences de Nancy, 1847, p. 182. Published as a separate book in 1859.
[8] Verh. d. Naturh. Ver. d. Preus. Rhein, *Ueber Beständigkeit und Umwandlung der Arten*, Bonn, 1853.
[9] *Études s. l. Geographie Botanique de l'Europe*, Paris, 1854, p. 199.

The Embryologists.

Let us first glance at the embryologists. MECKEL (1781–1833) followed Wolff (1735–1794) in the series of German founders of Embryology. Wolff had emphasized the transmutations of structure, so that, from seeds on the one side and eggs on the other, came the many and diverse organisms. Meckel more clearly anticipated Von Baer in 1811, in the passage: "There is no good physiologist who has not been struck, incidentally, by the observation that the original form of all organisms is one and the same, and that out of this one form, all, the lowest as well as the highest, are developed in such a manner that the latter pass through the permanent forms of the former as transitory stages."

VON BAER, in 1834, in a lecture entitled "The Most General Laws of Nature in all Development," maintained that: "Only in a very childish view of Nature could species be regarded as permanent and unchangeable types, and that, in fact, they can be only passing series of generations, which have developed by transmission from the common original form." (See Haeckel, Vol. I., p. 112.) SERRES, in his *Précis d'Anatomie Transcendente* (1842, p. 135), enlarged the arguments of Meckel, and showed that the missing links in the chain of Evolution may all be discovered, if we seek them, in the life of the embryo. When we compare animals arrived at their complete development, we find many differences between them; but if we compare them during their successive stages of Evolution, we see that these differences were preceded by resemblances; that, in fact, Comparative Anatomy is an arrested embryology, and Embryology is a transitory comparative anatomy.

The Followers of Buffon.

Among those who took up, more especially, the ideas of Buffon and Linnæus, was the Rev. W. Herbert, in his work on the '*Amaryllidaceæ*,' 1837,[1] in which he declares that "horticultural experiments have established, beyond the possibility of refutation, that botanical species are only a higher and more permanent class of varieties"; that single species of each genus were created in an originally plastic condition, and that these had produced, by intercrossing and by variation, all our existing species. He thus takes a point midway between Linnæus and Buffon.

Another Buffonian was CHRISTIAN LEOPOLD VON BUCH (1773-1853), a well-known naturalist and geologist. In 1836 he published an essay entitled, "Physical Description of the Canary Islands." We find that he is struck, like Humboldt, with the problem raised by the geographical distribution of plants; unlike the great traveller, he does not hesitate, but proceeds to solve it. He says:—

[1] See also the fourth volume of the *Horticultural Transactions*, 1822.

"The individuals of genera on continents spread and widely diffuse themselves; owing to differences of localities, nourishment, and soil, they form varieties; and in consequence of their isolation and never being crossed by other varieties and so brought back to the main type, they, in the end, become a permanent and distinct species. Then, perhaps, in other ways, they meet with other descendants of the original form, — which have likewise become new varieties, — and both now become distinct species, no longer mingling with one another. Not so on islands. Being commonly confined in narrow valleys, or within the limits of small zones, individuals can reach one another and destroy every commencing production of a permanent variety."

We find in Von Buch a clear conception of the force of Isolation or Segregation, which had been observed by Buffon, as we have seen; his theory of Evolution is also that of the direct action of environment, advocated by Buffon and St. Hilaire.

In 1844 (*Bost. Journ. Nat. Hist.*, 1843–44), HALDEMAN gave a full discussion of the arguments for and against the 'Lamarckian hypothesis,' in a paper entitled "Enumeration of the Recent Fresh-water Mollusca which are Common to North America and Europe." He wrote, apparently, from Lyell's exposition of Lamarck, rather than from the original author himself. He inclined strongly to the transmutation theory, although hesitating to offer a direct opinion. As to the causes of modification, he ignores Lamarck's special theory, and tends rather to adopt Buffon's factor of the direct action of the environment.

HERBERT SPENCER appeared as one of the few

out-and-out evolutionists before the publication of the *Origin of Species*. In his articles, "Illogical Geology"[1] and "The Development Hypothesis," he strongly contrasts the difficulties of the Special Creation hypothesis with the arguments for development. He does not enter into the question of the factors of Evolution, although such passages as the following might be interpreted as showing his inclination to Buffon's theory: ". . . Any existing species, animal or vegetable, when placed under conditions different from its previous ones, immediately begins to undergo certain changes of structure fitting it for the new conditions. . . . There is at work a modifying influence of the kind they assign as the cause of these specific differences."

THE PROGRESSIONISTS.

The Vestiges of the Natural History of Creation appeared in England, in 1844, — the only volume wholly devoted to Evolution between the *Philosophie Zoologique*, and the *Origin of Species*. It was published anonymously, but is now attributed to ROBERT CHAMBERS (1802–1871), because of his liberal views and considerable knowledge of Geology; yet he never acknowledged the authorship which still remains unclaimed. Although intelligently and reverently written, it met a scathing reception from the reviewers upon the score of false science and

[1] These articles were republished in 1865, in an American edition of *Spencer's Essays*, entitled, "Illustrations of Universal Progress."

infidelity. We may, in part, excuse the author for preserving the somewhat invalorous *incognito*, when we read in the *North British Review:* " Prophetic of infidel times, and indicating the unsoundness of our general education, the *Vestiges* has started into public favour with a fair chance of poisoning the fountains of science, and sapping the foundations of religion." The great sensation which this book caused, and its rapid sale, through ten editions in nine years, is proof that the truth of Evolution was ready to burst forth like a volcano, and that the times were ready for Darwin. The volume was the strongest presentation of the scientific evidences for Cosmic Evolution *versus* Special Creation which had appeared. We find that the author begins with the solar system; his middle point is the origin of life from inorganic matter, and his final point is man as last in the development of the animal kingdom. Of man's origin, he says: —

"But the idea that any of the lower animals have been concerned in any way in the origin of man — is not this degrading? Degrading is a term expressive of a notion of the human mind, and the human mind is liable to prejudices which prevent its notions from being invariably correct. . . . It has pleased Providence to arrange that one species should give birth to another, until the second highest gave birth to man, who is the very highest: be it so, it is our part to admire and to submit."

The work shows the author's familiarity with Buffon, Erasmus Darwin, Lamarck, St. Hilaire, and Serres. In the first edition (p. 174), he rejects Lamarck's hypothesis, "which has incurred much ridicule and scarcely ever had a single defender," on the ground that the arbitrary modification of form by the needs of the animal could never have led to the unities and analogies of structure which we observe. On the previous page, he advocates (without credit) St. Hilaire's modification of Buffon's hypothesis of the direct action of environment. Light, heat, the chemical constitution of the atmosphere, he says, "may have been the immediate prompting cause of all those advances from species to species which we have seen, upon other grounds, to be necessarily supposed as having taken place"; he continues that these ideas are merely thrown out as hints towards the formation of a just hypothesis which will come with advancing knowledge. He considers these natural laws as instruments in working out and realizing all the forms of being of the original Divine Conception. These views were more definitely expressed in the tenth edition, which appeared in 1853 (p. 155). Here he gives as his final opinion that the animal series is the result, *first*, of an *impulse*, imparted by God, advancing all the forms of life, through the various grades of organization, from the lowest to the highest plants and animals. (This is the Aristotelian 'internal perfecting principle' somewhat disguised.) As this first 'perfecting' impulse would evidently produce types not fitted to their environment, the author adds a *second impulse*, tending to modify organic structures in accordance with their environment, food, nature of the habitat, meteoric agencies, and thus to produce the 'adaptations' of the natural theologian.

This progressive advance with modification would also leave a gap at the bottom of the scale; to fill this up, the author, like Lamarck, supposes that there is a continuous spontaneous generation of the lowest forms of life, of primordial nucleated vesicles, the meeting-point between the organic and inorganic; this generation he believes to be an electro-chemical operation.

The author has been aptly termed a 'progressionist,' because of his belief in the internal perfecting or 'progressing' principle. Owen, and in a measure Louis Agassiz, should also be classed as 'progressionists.'

RICHARD OWEN (1810-1892), whose recent death marked the last of the old school, was the leading comparative anatomist of the world in the period after Cuvier, with whom he studied.

He was not, however, a scientific successor of Cuvier in a strict sense, but followed also St. Hilaire and Oken in Philosophical Anatomy and in a guarded acceptance of the transmutation theory. From Oken and Goethe he developed his famous, but now wholly discarded, theory of the skull, as derived from the modifications of vertebræ; the idea of archetypal or perfect type forms as ancestral to modern, degenerate, or vestigial types, seems also to have been his central thought in connection with Evolution. The vast range of his knowledge in Comparative Anatomy and Osteology brought within his view series of structures in all stages of usefulness, and especially those which were transitory or vestigial in existing species, and persistent or well-developed in extinct species. Thus in his essay on "The Nature of Limbs," in 1849, he wrote: "The archetypal idea was manifested long prior to the existence of those animal species that actually exemplify it"; and in the same work we find the following passage: "To what natural laws or secondary causes the orderly succession and progression of species may have been committed, we are, as yet, ignorant." Again, in 1858, in his address before the British Association, he spoke of the axiom "of the continuous operation of creative power, or ordained becoming of living things,"—indicating that his belief in the discovery of natural law was limited by his belief in the continuous operation of the supernatural law. He cited the Apteryx of New Zealand especially, with its excessively degenerate wings, as shaking our confidence in the theory of Special Creation. It thus appears that, prior to the publication of Darwin's work, Owen was an evolutionist in a limited degree, somewhat in the manner of Buffon; that is, in holding to the production of many modern species by modification, chiefly in the line of degeneration from older and more perfect types. There is no evidence whatever that he was an evolutionist in the large, comprehensive sense of Lamarck.

Upon the publication of the *Origin of Species*, Owen took an unfortunate position of hostility to the evidences for the natural factors of Evolution which Darwin sought to establish, and at the same time claimed that he had long held a belief in transmutation. In the preface of his *Anatomy of Vertebrates*, published in 1866, we find the following sentence: "Therefore, with every disposition to acquire information and receive instruction, as to how species become such, I am still compelled, as in 1849, to confess ignorance of the mode of operation of the natural law or secondary cause of their succession on the earth. But that it is an 'orderly succession,' or according to law, and also 'progressive,' or in the ascending course, is evident from actual knowledge of extinct species." He then goes on to say that the basis of belief in the succession and progression of species was laid by the demonstration of the unity of plan as shown in special and general homologies (Vicq d'Azyr and St. Hilaire), by comparison of embryonic stages of higher animals with the adult forms of lower animals (Meckel, Von Baer), by the succession of species in time. He concludes: "How inherited, or what may be the manner of operance of the secondary cause in the production of species, remains in the hypothetical state exemplified by the guess-endeavours of Lamarck, Darwin, Wallace, and others."

This attitude of hostility towards modern Evolution was apparently maintained throughout Owen's life, and although he outlived Darwin, I am not aware that he ever published his acceptance of the theory. In some of his lectures he is said to have held that a limited degree of degeneration is due to disuse.

THE SELECTIONISTS.

The modern theory of Natural Selection was expressed first by DR. W. C. WELLS, in 1813, then by St. Hilaire the elder, then by Matthew, in 1831, and finally, with considerably less clearness, if at all, by Naudin, in 1852. Darwin gives us references to the two English writers. That of Wells is the first statement of the theory of the survival, not simply of fittest organisms, as understood by previous writers, such as Buffon and Treviranus, but of organisms surviving because of their possession of favourable variations in single characters. Wells' paper, read before the Royal Society in 1813, was entitled, "An Account of a White Female, part of whose Skin resembles that of a Negro"; it was not published until 1818.[1] He here recognizes the principle of Natural Selection, as applied to the races

[1] See his *Two Essays upon the Dew and Single Vision*.

of men, and to the explanation of the origin of single characters. In Darwin's words:—

"After remarking that negroes and mulattoes enjoy an immunity from certain tropical diseases, he observes, firstly, that all animals tend to vary in some degree, and, secondly, that agriculturists improve their domesticated animals by selection; and then, he adds, but what is done in this latter case by art seems to be done with equal efficacy, though more slowly, by Nature, in the formation of varieties of mankind, fitted for the country which they inhabit. Of the accidental varieties of man, which would occur among the first few and scattered inhabitants of the middle regions of Africa, some one would be better fitted than the others to bear the diseases of the country. This race would consequently multiply, while the others would decrease; not only from their inability to sustain the attacks of disease, but from their incapacity of contending with their more vigorous neighbours. The colour of this vigorous race I take for granted, from what has been already said, would be dark. But the same disposition to form varieties still existing, a darker and a darker race would in the course of time occur; and as the darkest would be the best fitted for the climate, this would at length become the most prevalent, if not the only race, in the particular country in which it had originated."

This is certainly the most complete of all the anticipations of Darwinism.

In 1831 PATRICK MATTHEW published a work entitled *Naval Timber and Arboriculture*. It contained, in an appendix, a brief statement of a theory of the origin of species of which Darwin says: "The differences of Mr. Matthew's views from mine are not of much importance. He seems to consider that the world was nearly depopulated at successive periods, and then restocked, and he gives as an alternative, that 'new forms may be generated without the presence of any mould or germ of former aggregates.' I am not sure that I understand some passages; but it seems that he attributes some influence to the direct action of the conditions of life. He clearly saw, however, the full force of the principle of Natural Selection." Mr. Matthew was not satisfied with this handsome recognition of his priority; and is said to have placed on a subsequent title-page, after his name, " Discoverer of the principle of Natural Selection."

CHARLES NAUDIN, a veteran French botanist, is the last of the French precursors of Darwin. He followed Lamarck in the general transmutation doctrine, although he offered quite a different theory of the causes of transmutation. In an article entitled " Philosophical Considerations upon Species and Varieties," in the *Revue Horticole* (1852, p. 102), Naudin put forth his views upon the origin of species, which were published with some reluctance by the editors of that journal, because of their heretical character, transmutation then being at the height of its unpopularity. Quatrefages has outlined Naudin's views very carefully, yet we cannot perceive with him any evidence that Naudin understood the selection theory. Naudin does not speculate upon the origin of life. He bases his belief in transmutation upon 'unity of type,' as proof, not of a preconceived plan, but of a common parentage. From common sources existing species have issued through long intermediate series, and the sum of their analogies and differences represents their greater or less remoteness from each other and from the common source. From relatively few primordial types, Nature has given birth to all the organisms which people the globe. He quite literally follows Lamarck's conception of filiation as a branching system, but he widely departs from Lamarck as to the causes of Evolution. With Goethe, he sees in living organisms a '*plasticity*,' which renders them susceptible to direct modification by environment and opposes the conservative power of Atavism, or hereditary transmission of type. As with Bory de St. Vincent, he believes that the younger primitive types presented greater 'plasticity,' but with advancing ages the forces of heredity accumulated and became stronger.

Behind that 'plasticity' and 'Atavism,' however, Naudin places a higher power, — '*Finality*,' — a mysterious force, which, he says, some would call 'fatality' and others 'providence,' the continuous action of which upon beings determines the form, size, and duration of each species in relation to the order of things of which it forms a part. The natural species is a product, then, of Atavism and of Finality. By Finality, Naudin evidently does not imply an internal perfecting tendency in Nature, but rather a continuous controlling principle above the reign of secondary causes. Naudin evidently felt the need of something behind Natural Law in the production of the adaptations of Nature. The following most interesting passage in Naudin's paper, quoted below, is that in which Quatrefages and Varigny believe that this author anticipated the theory of Natural Selection:—

"We do not think that Nature has made her species in a different fashion from that in which we proceed ourselves in order to make our variations. To tell the truth, we have practised her very method. When we wish, out of some zoölogical or botanical species, to obtain a variety which answers to such or such of our needs, we select (*choisissons*) out of the large number of the individuals of this species, so as to make them the starting-point of a new stirp, those which seem already to depart from the specific type in the direction which suits us; and by a rational and continuous sorting of the descendants, after an undetermined number of generations, we create types or artificial species, which correspond more or less with the ideal type we had imagined, and which transmit the acquired characters to their descendants in proportion to the number of generations upon which our efforts have been bearing. Such is, in our opinion, the method followed by Nature, as well as by ourselves. She has wished to create races conformable to her needs; and with a comparatively small number of primitive types, she has successively, and at different periods, given birth to all the animal and vegetable species which people the earth." . . .

We cannot find in this passage clear proof of anticipation of Darwinism.[1] The Survival of the Fittest, as due to the possession of favourable variations, was evidently not in Naudin's mind; still less

[1] This was Darwin's opinion after carefully studying Naudin's paper in 1859: "I declare I cannot see a *much* closer approach to Wallace and me in Naudin than in Lamarck,—we all agree in modification and descent. . . . But I cannot find one word like the struggle for Existence and Natural Selection." (*Life and Letters*, 1st ed. II., p. 247.)

is it in his system of Evolution as explained above. A very careful reading of this passage shows that in the comparison of methods pursued by man and by Nature, his emphasis is plainly not upon the natural selection but upon the natural succession of types. Man causes types to succeed each other artificially; Nature also causes types to succeed each other; he does not say that Nature selects the fittest types. A single passage like this is often very misleading; we must always study the author's whole context. A century earlier Buffon had much more clearly expressed the idea of the survival of the fittest species of plants.

In 1855 appeared an article[1] by ALFRED RUSSEL WALLACE, "On the Law which has regulated the Introduction of New Species." This contains a very strong argument for the theory of descent, as explaining the facts of classification, of distribution, and of succession of species in geological time during the great changes upon the earth. Wallace at this time showed himself a strong and fearless evolutionist, although he had not apparently arrived at his subsequent theory of the causes of change.

STATE OF OPINION IN THE MID-CENTURY.

In all that has passed in these lectures the anti-evolutionists have been kept in the background. Yet

[1] *Annals and Magazine of Natural History*, September, 1855. Republished in 1870 in *Contributions to the Theory of Natural Selection. A Series of Essays.* Macmillan & Co., London.

they formed the great working majority in numbers and influence. By considering only the evolutionists, we have wholly lost the perspective of opinion in the mid-century. This perspective must be regained in order to appreciate the revolution of thought brought about by Darwin.

Lyell, who believed in Natural Causation as part of his doctrine of Uniformity, had been teaching that, "as often as certain forms of animals and plants disappeared, for reasons quite unintelligible to us, others took their place by virtue of a causation, which was quite beyond our comprehension." He had carefully studied, and rejected, the Lamarckian explanation. The very apologetic tone in which Darwin himself confessed to Hooker, Lyell, and Gray, in turn, his nascent belief in the mutability of species, proves that he did not consider this belief as an enviable or altogether desirable possession. "I formerly spoke," he wrote, "to very many naturalists on the subject of Evolution, and never once met with any sympathetic agreement. It is probable that some did then believe in Evolution, but they were either silent, or expressed themselves so ambiguously, that it was not easy to understand their meaning." Later, after the completion of the *Origin*, he wrote: "If I can only convince Hooker, Lyell, and Huxley that species are mutable"; again, in reply to Huxley's somewhat guarded acceptance of the theory: "like a good Catholic who has received extreme unction, I can now sing '*nunc dimittis*.'"

Think now of convincing this high priest of Evolution. In America, Asa Gray was one of the first to espouse Darwin's cause.

In France, which we have found to be the home of the modern theory for nearly a century, Evolution came as an unwelcome returning exile. As in England, opinion had finally become settled upon the fixity of species. A proffered translation of the *Origin* was contemptuously rejected by a publishing firm in Paris. Darwin craved an open-minded audience, which was almost impossible to find on the Continent. " Do you know of any good and speculative foreigners to whom it would be worth while to send my book ? " he wrote to Huxley. This is all by way of evidence of the well-known fact that all the progress which had been made in the long centuries we have been considering was, for the time, a latent force. The Evolution idea, with the numerous truths which had accumulated about it, was again almost wholly subordinate to the Special Creation idea.

Darwin.

It is impossible to give Darwin his true relief in the brief limits of these outlines, that is, in proportion to his actual work and influence, as compared with his predecessors, and it is difficult to say anything about him which has not been better said before. We can, however, ask two questions which

connect him with this history, and can be brought
into a stronger light than has been done hitherto.
First, how much did Darwin owe to the evolutionists who went before him? Second, what was the
course of his own changing opinion upon the
factors of Evolution?

As to the first, he owed far more to the past than
is generally believed, or than he himself was conscious of, especially to the full and true conception
of the Evolution idea, which had already been
reached, to the nature of its evidences, and, to some
extent, to the line of its factors. Although anticipated by others, Darwin conceived, and worked
out, the theory of Natural Selection. What he
owed to no one came from his genius and his wonderful application of the inductive method of search
after natural laws. Like Lamarck alone, among all
his predecessors, Darwin was early fired with the
truth of the idea and was equally ready to suffer
social and scientific ostracism in its pursuit.

Second, I will endeavour to trace the influences
which moulded Darwin's earlier and later opinions;
how, starting with some leaning towards the theories of modification of Buffon and Lamarck, he
reached an almost exclusive belief in his own theory,
and then gradually inclined to adopt Buffon's,
and then Lamarck's theories as well, until in his
maturest writings he embraced a threefold causation in the origin of species. Namely, as first and
most important, the Darwin-Wallace factor of

Natural Selection; second, as of considerable importance, the E. Darwin-Lamarck factor of the inheritance of the effects of use and disuse; third, as still of some importance, the Buffon factor of the direct action of the environment. Yet he reached each of these factors, not so much through the arguments advanced by their authors, as by his own and by contemporary observations.

All this connects Darwin with the past; not by way of diminishing his lustre, but of doing the past justice. And now a word as to the method which enabled him, in a single lifetime, to leap along over the progress of centuries. The long retention of his theory from publication marks the contrast of his caution with the impetuousness of Lamarck. He sought a hundred facts and observations where his predecessors had sought one; his notes filled volumes, and he stands out as the first evolutionist who worked 'upon true Baconian principles.' It was this characteristic which, combined with his originality, won the battle for the Evolution idea. As Canon Kingsley wrote to Maurice: "Darwin is conquering everywhere, and rushing in like a flood by the mere force of truth and fact." When the grandfather, Erasmus Darwin, held back at the inadequacy of his own theory to explain the origin of adaptation in colour, he displayed the rare scientific temper which he transmitted to the grandson. Krause has pointed out, what is in fact most obvious, how largely the thoughts of these elder and younger evolutionists of the same family ran in parallel lines. They seemed to have inborn tendencies to look at Nature in the same way.

Another cause of Darwin's success where all others had failed was his life at a time when the storehouse of facts was fairly bursting for want of a generalization; the progress in every branch since Lamarck's time had been prodigious. Again, even this combination of temperament and circumstance might have failed but for Darwin's rare education from Nature upon the voyage of the *Beagle*. He had gained little or nothing from the routine methods of education in school and university, as we learn in his own words: "My scientific tastes appear to have been certainly innate. . . . I consider that all I have learnt of any value has been self-taught. . . . My innate taste for natural history strongly confirmed and directed by the voyage of the *Beagle*." Humboldt's *Personal Narrative*, and Herschel's *Introduction to the Study of Natural Philosophy* aroused his enthusiasm. His natural taste for Geology, chilled by earlier teachers, was revived during an excursion with Professor Sedgwick, from whom he learned "that science consists in grouping facts so that general laws and conclusions may be drawn from them." This was in 1831; and upon his return he entered upon his 'Voyage.'

His training for such an undertaking had

been slight, and when we read what he *saw* during these three years, between the age of twenty-two and twenty-five, we realize the greatness of his genius. The procession of life in time had already come passingly before him. He now learnt for himself, first, the great lesson of uniformity of past and present causes, that for Nature 'time is nothing.' The rocks, the fossils, the life of the continents and islands passed before his mind like a panorama of that grand history which had come singly and in fragments to every evolutionist preceding him. Only a few decades back, Humboldt had taken a somewhat similar journey in South America, and had written: "This phenomenon" (the distribution of plants) "is one of the most curious in the history of organic forms. I say history, for in vain would reason *forbid man to form hypotheses upon the origin of things;* he still goes on puzzling himself with insoluble problems relating to the distribution of beings." The same phenomena came to Darwin's mind as the greatest and most pressing for solution, and he returned from this voyage determined to solve the problem of the origin of species by induction. There were but two theories to choose from, the Special Creation theory, and the Transmutation theory. He took them up with an open mind.

Now let us see how the full-grown Evolution idea had come to him. At the age of eighteen, while in the University of Edinburgh, Darwin formed the acquaintance of Dr. Grant, who, on one occasion, burst forth into high praise of the doctrines of Lamarck. Darwin had even earlier read the *Zoonomia*, but without receiving any effect from it. "Nevertheless," he says, "it is probable that the hearing, rather early in life, such views maintained and praised, may have favoured my upholding them in a different form in my *Origin of Species.*" It is very evident from all Darwin's criticisms of Lamarck that he never studied him carefully in the original, so that all he owed at this time to his grandfather and to Lamarck was the general idea of the evolution of life. Later, however, on the *Beagle*, he took with him Lyell's *Principles of Geology*, in which Lamarck's doctrines are admirably set forth and fully discussed, so that there is little doubt that the problem of transformation was, after all, most strongly brought to him by Lamarck indirectly through Lyell's able treatment. In 1834, during the voyage, Darwin was still a special creationist, yet the problem of mutability haunted him, as it was brought home by the strong evidences of change which met him on every side. He says:—

"I had been deeply impressed by the discovery in the Pampean collection of great fossil animals covered with armour, like that on the existing Armadillos; secondly, by the manner in which closely allied animals replaced one another in proceeding southwards over the Continent; and thirdly, by the South-American character of most of the products of the Galapagos Archipelago, and more especially by the manner in which they differed on each island of the group, none of the islands appearing to be very ancient in a geological sense. It was evident that such facts as these, as well as many others, could only be explained on the supposition that species gradually became modified; and the subject haunted me. But it was equally evident that neither the action of the surrounding conditions,[1] nor the will of the organisms[2] (especially in the case of plants), could account for the innumerable cases in which organisms of every kind are beautifully adapted to their habits of life; for instance, the woodpecker or the tree frog to climb trees, or a seed for dispersal, by hooks or plumes. I had always been much struck by such adaptations; and until these could be explained, it seemed to me almost useless to endeavour to prove by indirect evidence that species have been modified."

It was after his return in 1837 that Darwin opened his first note-book for the collection of facts which bore in any way on variation in animals and plants under domestication and in Nature. He says: "I worked on true Baconian principles, and without any theory collected facts on a wholesale scale, more especially with respect to domesticated products, by printed inquiries, by conversation with skilful breeders and gardeners, and by extensive reading." This is the most deliberate and rigid instance of the application of the inductive method which we have met with in our whole study of the contributors to the Evolution theory. Darwin soon saw the force of Selection as the secret of man's success in forming useful races of animals and plants; and in October, 1838, while reading Malthus on population, the idea of Selection in a state of Nature first occurred to him as the result of the

[1] He here refers to Buffon's factor.
[2] He here refers to and misconceives Lamarck's factor.

struggle for existence, or rather for life, between different individuals and species. Four years later he briefly set down his views, and in 1844 he allowed himself to write out his progress. He had already reached the main line of argument of his *Origin of Species*, including the now familiar tripod of his theory, Struggle, Variation, and Selection; also his principle of Sexual Selection, yet he attached much more weight to the influence of external conditions and to the inheritance of acquired habits than in the *Origin*[1] of 1859.

At this time Darwin naturally looked into the literature of the subject, and was reading Geoffroy St. Hilaire. He carefully read and abstracted Haldeman's arguments for and against the development theory. He studied De Candolle upon geographical distribution, and Brown upon variation. He was also fearful lest he should be classed with Lamarck. He wrote to Hooker (Jan. 11, 1844):—

" . . . I have now been, ever since my return, engaged in a very presumptuous work, and I know no one individual who would not say a very foolish one. I was so struck with the distribution of the Galapagos organisms, etc., and with the character of the American fossil mammifers, etc., that I determined to collect, blindly, every sort of fact, which could bear in any way on what are species. . . . At last, gleams of light have come, and I am almost convinced (quite contrary to the opinion that I started with) that species are not (it is like confessing a murder) immutable. Heaven forfend me from Lamarck nonsense of a 'tendency

[1] See *Life and Letters*, Vol. II., p. 14. This was Huxley's observation upon this essay in reply to a request for a criticism from the editor. This essay should be published.

to progression,' 'adaptations from the slow willing of animals,' etc.! But the conclusions I am led to are not widely different from his; though the means of change are wholly so." In another place he wrote: "Lamarck's work appeared to me to be extremely poor; I got not a fact or idea from it."

By 1856, Darwin had sent Hooker his manuscripts. He had also, as a matter of greatest interest to us in the development of his views, swung entirely away from any sympathy with the theories of Buffon and Lamarck, and had reached the extreme position as to the powers of Natural Selection which he continued to hold for some years. Several passages show this:—

" . . . External conditions (to which naturalists so often appeal) do, by themselves, very little. How much they do, is the point, of all others, on which I feel myself very weak. I judge from the facts of variation under domestication, and I may yet get more light. . . . The formation of a strong variety or species I look at as almost wholly due to the selection of what may be incorrectly called 'chance'[1] variations, or variability." As to the powers of Natural Selection, he wrote to Lyell, in 1859: "Grant a simple archetypal creature, like the Mud-fish or Lepidosiren, with the five senses and some vestige of mind, and *I believe Natural Selection will account for the production of every vertebrate animal.*"

He was more cautious in publication, for in the first edition of the *Origin of Species*, which appeared in the same year, he said: "I am convinced that Natural Selection has been the main, but not the exclusive, means of modification."

In the use of 'chance,' Darwin recalls to mind the

[1] His meaning in the use of the word 'chance' was not the ordinary one. See 6th edition of the *Origin*, p. 121: "I have sometimes spoken," etc.

old passage in Aristotle of the two alternatives in our views of Nature. Darwin's standpoint was different from either; by 'chance variations' he refers to those occurring under unknown laws, not under the 'blind fortuity' of Empedocles, nor under the 'progressive principle' of Aristotle. He found no evidence for an internal perfecting principle. In connection with the first edition of the *Origin*, he wrote: "The so-called improvement of our short-horn cattle, pigeons, etc., does not presuppose or require any aboriginal 'power of adaptation,' or 'principle of improvement.' If I have a second edition, I will reiterate 'Natural Selection,' and as a general consequence, 'Natural Improvement.'"

He mistakenly attributed to Lamarck the view held by the author of the *Vestiges*, when he disavowed holding "the Lamarckian or Vestigian doctrine of 'necessary progression,' that is, of progression independent of conditions." This is further shown in his correspondence concerning Nägeli. (*Life and Letters*, Vol. III., p. 49, letter to Victor Carus, 1866): "I am, however, far from agreeing with him that the acquisition of certain characters which appear to be of no service to plants, offers any great difficulty, or affords a proof of some innate tendency in plants towards perfection."[1] This standpoint

[1] Nägeli, a distinguished German botanist, believed that he found in his studies of the Evolution of plants, proofs of the existence of an internal perfecting principle in life, by which, independently of all outside agencies, the Plant Kingdom is constantly tending to a higher degree of perfection. These views were published in 1865. Somewhat similar views have been advanced by Baer, Kölliker, and others.

is further brought out in Darwin's very interesting correspondence with Asa Gray upon the evidence for Design in Nature: "I cannot think the world, as we see it, is the result of chance; and yet I cannot look at each separate thing as the result of Design. To take a crucial example, you lead me to infer that you believe 'that variation has been led along certain beneficial lines.' I cannot believe this."[1] Again: "I must think that it is illogical to suppose that the variations, which natural selection preserves for the good of any being, have been designed." In still another passage:[2] "I am inclined to look at everything as resulting from designed laws, with the details, whether good or bad, left to the working out of what we may call 'chance.' Not that this notion *at all* satisfies me."

This makes sufficiently clear Darwin's opinions at this time upon the theories of all his predecessors except one, namely, St. Hilaire. Huxley, in his early correspondence upon the *Origin of Species*, tried to convince Darwin of the possibility of occasional rapid leaps or changes in Nature, analogous to those which St. Hilaire had advocated, although Huxley probably did not have this author in mind nor contemplate any great extremes of transformation. Darwin held to his original proposition, handed down from Leibnitz: '*Natura non facit saltum*,' concluding: "It would take a great

---

[1] *Life and Letters*, Vol. II., p. 353, and p. 378.
[2] *Life and Letters*, Vol. II., p. 312.

deal more evidence to make me admit that forms have often changed *per saltum*."[1]

The idea of the Survival of the Fittest came to Darwin only through the suggestion of Malthus, who, in turn, probably borrowed it from Buffon. He was unaware of any of the distinct anticipations of his theory. His attention was called to Matthew's article in 1860; to that of Wells in 1865; to Naudin's paper in 1859. Some one, also, called his attention to Aristotle and Empedócles. It is possible that his eye may have caught the passage in St. Hilaire suggesting the idea, without his conscious recollection of it. The strong passage in Erasmus Darwin's poem may also have survived in his memory, yet as far as Darwin knew, the idea of the 'struggle for life' came first from Malthus; it grew upon him in reading De Candolle, W. Herbert, and Lyell, of whom he said, " Even they have not written strongly enough." The force of this 'struggle' gradually intensified itself in his mind to a point where he believed it was such that not merely the entire adaptive form of the animal, but even a slight adaptive variation in a single character, would turn the scale in favour of survival ! This was during the period of his extreme faith in the Natural Selection factor, which reached its highest point about 1858. He gradually receded from this extreme, as shown in a letter to Victor Carus in 1869: ". . . I have been led to infer

[1] *Life and Letters*, Vol. II., p. 274 (1860).

that single variations are of even less importance, in comparison with individual differences, than I formerly thought." He here refers to the aggregate of distinction between two forms.

This reaction was accompanied by a slow change of mind towards the Lamarckian factor of the inheritance of the effects of use and disuse. This was brought about, apparently, not through a renewed study of the *Philosophie Zoologique*, but by Darwin's own observations upon the domesticated animals, especially in his records of structures which were developing and degenerating entirely apart from the main course of the artificial selection of breeders, as well as from the weight of utility or usefulness in the scale of survival in Nature. He may have been influenced also by the thorough Lamarckism of Herbert Spencer, although this does not appear in the *Life and Letters*.

Darwin's gradual recession from his exclusion of the Buffon - St. Hilaire factor also evidently began in course of the preparation of his great work upon 'Variation.' He was influenced by his own wider range of observation, and, later, by the observations of Wagner, of Allen, and others. As early as 1862 he wrote to Lyell (*Life and Letters*, Vol. II., p. 390): —

"I hardly know why I am a little sorry, but my present work is leading me to believe rather more in the direct action of physical conditions. I presume I regret it, because it lessens the glory of Natural Selection, and is so confoundedly doubtful. Perhaps I shall change again when I get all my facts under one point of view, and a pretty hard job this will be."

Fourteen years later, Darwin had positively included Buffon's factor among the causes of Evolution. In 1876 he wrote to Moritz Wagner: —

"When I wrote the *Origin*, and for some years afterwards, I could find little good evidence of the direct action of the environment; now there is a large body of evidence, and your case of the Saturnia is one of the most remarkable of which I have heard."

In 1878 he fully included[1] Wagner's theory as one cause of origin of species, through the direct action of environment in the same country or through geographical isolation. In 1877 he also wrote to Morse: "I quite agree about the high value of Mr. Allen's works, as showing how much change may be expected apparently through the direct action of the conditions of life." There is thus no doubt that the idea of Natural Selection, as almost the sole factor, came to a climax in Darwin's mind and then gradually appeared less important and exclusive. In preparing his work on 'Variation,' the importance of the problem of heredity came before him, and in writing to Huxley, in 1865,[2] he gives a 'brief' of his point of view at the time, in concisely stating what a working theory of heredity should embrace: —

"The case stands thus: in my next book I shall publish long chapters on bud and seminal-variation, on inheritance, reversion,

[1] Letter to Semper, *Life and Letters*, Vol. III., p. 160.
[2] *Life and Letters*, Vol. III., p. 44.

effects of use and disuse, etc. I have also, for many years, speculated on the different forms of reproduction. Hence it comes to be a passion with me to try to connect all such facts by some sort of hypothesis."

Here, again, Darwin reached independently an hypothesis which had been already formulated by Buffon, Maupertuis, and foreshadowed by Democritus and Hippocrates. Concerning Buffon's unexpected anticipation, he wrote to Huxley, to whom he had submitted his manuscript:—

"I have read Buffon: whole pages are laughably like mine. It is surprising how candid it makes one to see one's views in another man's words. . . . Nevertheless, there is a fundamental distinction between Buffon's views and mine. He does not suppose that each cell or atom of tissue throws off a little bud. . . ."

Among Darwin's last words upon the factors of Evolution are those in the sixth edition of the *Origin of Species* (1880, p. 424). In the modification of species he refers as causes, successively to his own, to Lamarck's, and to Buffon's factor in the following clear language: "This has been effected chiefly through the natural selection of numerous, successive, slight, favourable variations; aided in an important manner by the inherited effects of the use and disuse of parts; and in an unimportant manner — that is in relation to adaptive structures whether past or present — by the direct action of external conditions, and by variations which seem to us in our ignorance to arise spontaneously." Later in the *Nature* of May 1881.

p. 32), he speaks of the effects of use as *probably* becoming hereditary, showing that he still did not consider the evidence as convincing as that relating to disuse (*loc. cit.*, p. 32). " The chief agents in causing organs to become rudimentary seem to have been disuse, at that period of life when the organ is chiefly used (and this is generally during maturity), and also inheritance at a corresponding period of life." It should be repeated that these decided changes of opinion were, in part, a tacit acceptance of work done elsewhere, especially in Germany, rather than the direct outcome of Darwin's own observations. In part they certainly reflected his own observations and maturer judgment.

Darwin and Wallace.

Finally, we record the most striking of all the many coincidences and independent discoveries in the history of the Evolution idea. Darwin's long retention of his theory from publication between 1837 and 1858 came near costing him his eminent claims to priority; for in the latter year Alfred Russel Wallace had also reached a similar theory. By the happy further coincidence of a friendship, which always remained of the most generous order, Wallace sent his freshly completed manuscript to Darwin. But for his friends Hooker and Lyell, Darwin would even then have held back his work. By their co-operation, two modest papers appeared in the *Journal of the Linnæan Society*, June 30, 1858, the first consisting of an abstract of Darwin's manuscripts of 1839 and 1844, from the second part, entitled "On the Variation of Organic Beings in a State of Nature; on the Natural Means of Selection; on the Comparison of Domestic Races and True Species"; also the letter of 1857 to Asa Gray. The second consisted of the paper by Wallace, written in February, 1858, entitled "On the Tendency of Varieties to depart indefinitely from the Original Type."

The line of thought in these two papers is almost directly parallel, as shown in these columns:—

DARWIN.	WALLACE.
There is in Nature a struggle for existence, as shown by Malthus and De Candolle.	The life of wild animals is a struggle for existence . . . in which the weakest and least perfect must always succumb.
Rapid multiplication, if unchecked, even of slow-breeding animals like the elephant . . .	Even the least prolific of animals would increase rapidly if unchecked.
Great changes in the environment occur.	A change in the environment may occur.
It has been shown in a former part of this work that such changes of external conditions would, from their acting upon the reproductive system, probably cause the organization . . . to become plastic.	(No cause of variation assigned.) Varieties do frequently occur spontaneously.
Can it be doubted that . . . any minute variation in structure, habits, or instincts, adapting that individual better to the new conditions, would tell upon its vigour and health?	All variations from the typical form have some definite effect, however slight, on the habits or capacities of the individuals. Abundance or rarity of a species is dependent on its more or less

In the struggle it would have a better *chance* of surviving; and those of the offspring who inherited the variation, be it ever so slight, would also have a better chance.

perfect adaptation. If any species should produce a variety having slightly increased powers of preserving existence, that variety must inevitably in time acquire a superiority in numbers.

Remarkable as this parallelism[1] is, it is not complete. The line of argument is the same, but the *point d'appui* is different. Darwin dwells upon *variations in single characters*, as taken hold of by Selection; Wallace mentions variations, but dwells upon *full-formed varieties*, as favourably or unfavourably adapted. It is perfectly clear that with Darwin the struggle is so intense that the chance of survival of each individual turns upon a single and even slight variation. With Wallace, Varieties are already presupposed by causes which he does not discuss, a change in the environment occurs, and those varieties which happen to be adapted to it survive. There is really a wide gap between these two statements and applications of the theory.

Unlike Darwin, Wallace has conserved his earlier views entire; he is still a rigid Natural Selectionist, and has incorporated the extreme views of Darwin upon the importance of variations in single characters. As one of the leaders of thought in contemporary Evolution, Wallace belongs chiefly to the after-Darwin period.

[1] A further striking feature in this parallelism of thought is that Wallace, like Darwin, first caught the suggestion of the struggle for existence from reading Malthus.

Retrospect.

Now that we have brought together the evidences, our difficulty lies in choosing the *via media* between an overestimate and an underestimate of actual continuity.

From the 'formless masses' of the thought of Empedocles we have traced Evolution to its perfect expression by Darwin. The metaphysical environment of the idea has been seen shaping itself in the better understanding of the relations of Causation, Design, and Creation, while the natural environment has been seen expanding with the biological sciences. Two of Aristotle's principles, midway between physics and metaphysics, seem to have exerted a great and often misleading influence. I refer first to his 'perfecting tendency' which led Leibnitz and all his naturalist and speculative followers away from the search for a natural cause of Adaptation; and second, his 'unity of type,' which, as finally developed in the mind of St. Hilaire and Owen, proved to be a compromise between Special Creation and Evolution.

The idea of Evolution, rooted in the cosmic evolution and 'movement' of Heraclitus and Aristotle, has passed to the progressive development and succession of life seen in Empedocles, Aristotle, Bruno, Descartes, Goethe, and in the more concrete 'mutability of species' of Bacon, Leibnitz, Buffon, Lamarck, and St. Hilaire.

The direct transition from the inorganic to the organic is seen to have had a host of friends, nearly to the present time, including, besides all the Greeks, Lucretius, Augustine, Maillet, Buffon, Erasmus Darwin, Lamarck, Treviranus, Oken, and Chambers. Then we have seen the difficulty of 'origin' removed one step back by the 'pre-existent germs' of Anaxagoras, revived by Maillet, Robinet, Didérôt, and Bonnet. Again, the rudiments of the monistic idea of the psychic properties of all matter, foreshadowed by Empedocles, are seen revived by Maupertuis and Didérôt. The difficulty of origin has been avoided by the assumption of primordial minute masses, which we have seen developed from the 'soft germ' of Aristotle, to the 'vesicles' and 'filaments' of Buffon, Erasmus Darwin, Lamarck, Oken, and finally into our primordial protoplasm.

To the inquiry: Where did life first appear? we find the answer, 'in the sea,' given by Thales, Anaximander, and Maillet; 'between sea and land,' is the answer of Anaximenes, Diogenes, Democritus, and Oken; 'from the earth,' is the solitary reply of Lucretius. Now we are too wise to answer it. For the succession of life we have followed the 'ascending scale' of Aristotle, Bruno, Leibnitz, and others, until Buffon realized its inadequacy, and Lamarck substituted the simile of the branching tree. Of man as the summit of the scale, and still in process of becoming more perfect in his endowments, we learn from Empedocles, Aristotle, Robinet, Diderôt, Erasmus Darwin, Lamarck, and Treviranus.

Man's origin and descent has always been of the first interest to man himself. The idea of his slow development is suggested by the crude observation of Anaximander, and takes its more scientific form in Lucretius, Bruno, and Leibnitz. Man's relation to other primates as a result of evolution is developed by Bruno, Leibnitz, Buffon, Kant, Herder. Bruno perceives the importance of the tool-bearing hands, and most interesting is the appreciation by Buffon, Helvetius, and Erasmus Darwin, that the opposition of the thumb, rendering its bearers fittest to survive, may have originated as a happy accident.

Of the greatest moment of all, is our pursuit of the problem of Adaptation as it first presented itself to Empedocles, Democritus, Anaxagoras; and second, as it became connected with Causation in the minds of Aristotle, Buffon, Kant, Erasmus Darwin, Goethe, and Charles Darwin. Around the solution of this problem we have seen centre the development of four conceptions; namely, of 'environment,' 'struggle for existence,' 'variation,' and 'survival of the fittest.'

We have seen first how ideas of Adaptation in immutable types were recast into the grander Adaptation in mutable types under changing environment; also how the full modern conception of Adaptation slowly arose through philosophical

Anatomy and Embryology, as pursued by Buffon, Kant, Erasmus Darwin, Lamarck, Goethe, Treviranus, St. Hilaire, and Serres. The significance of 'degeneration' and of 'vestigial structures' meanwhile grew clear in the interpretations of Sylvius, Buffon, Kant, Goethe, and Lamarck.

'Environment' as a transforming factor was apparently observed late, for we have seen it first develop in the writings of Bacon, Maillet, Buffon, Kant, Erasmus Darwin, Lamarck, Treviranus, St. Hilaire, St. Vincent, Buch, and others. The 'struggle for existence' we have traced to Anaximander, and more clearly in its bearing upon feeding and propagation, to Empedocles and Lucretius. Buffon and Malthus greatly developed it afresh, while Erasmus Darwin, Treviranus, De Candolle, and others gave it its modern form. 'Variation' is of seventeenth century origin, at least when considered partly as evidence of, partly as a factor in, Evolution; we have seen it treated by Bacon, Leibnitz, Maupertuis, Lamarck, and St. Hilaire, terminating with its full exposition in the first half of the century as a link of Darwinism.

The broad conception of fortuitous combinations and of accidental variations in relation to Survival and hence to Adaptation, is found to be one of the most ancient scientific ideas of which we have record in history. It is seen to follow two lines. The first is the survival of the fittest forms or types of life, considered as a whole, as a collection of similar individuals, or as a 'variety' in modern terms. This we have seen originate with Empedocles and receive the support of Epicurus and Lucretius, and much more recently of Hume, Diderôt, and others. In its relation to modern Evolution, we see it brought out afresh by Buffon, Malthus, Kant, Wells, Matthew, and Wallace. The second line is the survival of certain types, because of the possession of some fortuitously adaptive combination of parts or of some favourable variation in a single organ. This conception we also trace from Diderôt back to Empedocles; but it is apparently a spontaneous and independent discovery as we find it in Buffon and Helvetius, who transmit it to Erasmus Darwin. Finally, it is again rediscovered, or grandly evolved by induction and observation by Charles Darwin, who raises it to its present magnitude as a central principle in the living world.

An entirely distinct line of thought is that of Erasmus Darwin and of Lamarck that life itself is a process of adaptation to new conditions and that the adaptive changes acquired in course of life are transmitted and accumulated in successive generations. This is a theory for adaptations of certain kinds which awaits further proof.

It is also for the future to determine whether the predecessors of Darwin and Darwin himself, in the principle to which he gave a life of thought, have fully answered the old, old problem, or whether we shall look for still another Newton in our philosophy of Nature.

BIBLIOGRAPHY.

For the general succession of evolutionists, in Philosophy especially, the student is referred to Huxley in his article "Evolution" in the *Encyclopædia Britannica*, to Haeckel in his *History of Creation*, and to Schultze in his *Philosophie der Naturwissenschaft*. Upon the long discussion of the problem of the mutability of species which occurred between the time of Linnæus and of St. Hilaire, by far the best work is Isidore St. Hilaire's *Histoire Naturelle Générale*. I have also depended largely upon the full and critical studies of the French evolutionists by Perrier, Quatrefages, Martins, Varigny, Lanessan. The German natural philosophers and poets have been explored for their Evolution tendencies in special studies by Schultze, Bärenbach, and Haeckel. Goethe especially has been searched with rich results. We owe to Germany, also, Krause's *Life of Erasmus Darwin*. To the English writers we owe the articles already mentioned, a number of biographies in the Britannica, Darwin's outline in his introduction of the *Origin of Species*, F. Darwin's *Life and Letters of Charles Darwin*, and the vigorous interchange of opinions upon Evolution in theological literature between Huxley and Mivart. In this country Packard has contributed an article to the *Standard Natural History*, but Lamarckism in America is a subject which still deserves careful study.

Zeller has given us the most critical and reliable studies of the early or pre-Aristotelian Greek evolutionists. For the later Greek period, I have referred to the general works of Lange and Erdmann; and to the special studies of Cotterill, Moore, Güttler, Brunnhofer, and others for the later Greek and Mediæval period. Lewes' *Aristotle* is a mine of information, yet the author strangely enough wholly fails to appreciate or bring forward Aristotle's important contributions to the Evolution idea. In fact, Aristotle has been generally ignored in this connection.

General Articles and Works.

ISIDORE GEOFFROY SAINT-HILAIRE: 'Histoire Naturelle Générale des Règnes Organiques.' Paris, 1844-1862. 3 vols.
HUXLEY, THOMAS H.: 'Evolution.' Enc. Britannica, Vol. VIII., pp. 744-772.
HAECKEL, ERNST: 'Natürliche Schöpfungsgeschichte.' 1st ed., 1868. 4th ed., 'The History of Creation' (translation), 1892. 2 vols.
ERDMANN: 'History of Philosophy.' 3 vols. Swann, Sonnenschein & Co., London.
LANGE: 'History of Materialism.'
FISKE: 'Outlines of Cosmic Philosophy.'
SCHULTZE, FRITZ: 'Philosophie der Naturwissenschaft.' Leipsic, 1881. 2 vols.
PACKARD, A. S.: Introduction to the 'Standard Natural History.' Boston, 1885.

The Greek Period.

ZELLER, EDWARD: 'History of the Greek Philosophy.'
    'Ueber die Griechischen Vorgänger Darwin's.' Abhand. d. Berliner Akad., 1878, p.
LEWES, G. H.: 'Aristotle; a Chapter in the History of Science.' London, 1864.
ARISTOTLE, Works of. Taylor's translation. 6 vols.
G. POUCHET: 'La Biologie Aristotélique.' Paris, 1885.
ROMANES, GEORGE J.: 'Aristotle as a Naturalist.' Contemporary Review, 1891.
COTTERILL, HENRY: 'Does Science aid Faith in Regard to Creation?' London, 1883.
MOORE, AUBREY: 'Science and Faith.'
GÜTTLER, C.: 'Lorenz Oken und sein Verhältniss zur Modernen Entwickelungslehre.' Leipsic, 1884.
BRUNNHOFER: 'Giordano Bruno's Welt Anschauung.' Leipsic, 1882.
HUXLEY, T. H.: 'Critiques and Addresses.' London, 1883.
MIVART, ST. GEORGE: 'On the Genesis of Species.' London, 1871.
    'Lessons from Nature.' London, 1876.

The Natural Philosophers and Speculative Evolutionists.

BACON: 'Novum Organum and Advancement of Learning.' Bohn Edition.
SCHULTZE, FRITZ: 'Kant und Darwin, ein Beitrag zur Geschichte der Entwickelungslehre.' Jena, 1875.
BÄRENBACH, FRIEDRICH VON: 'Herder als Vorgänger Darwin's und der Modernen Naturphilosophie.' Berlin, 1877.
DE MAUPERTUIS, PETER LOUIS MOREAU: 'Système de la Nature.' Paris, 1751.
DE MAILLET, M.: 'Telliamed ou Entretiens d'un Philosophe Indien sur la diminution de la Mer, avec un Missionaire Français.' Basle, 1749. 2eme ed. Paris, 1754. 2 vols.
LEWES, G. H.: 'A Precursor of the *Vestiges*.' (Robinet.) Fraser's Magazine, November, 1857, pp. 526-531.
ROBINET, J. B.: 'Considérations Philosophiques de la Gradation Naturelle des Formes de l'être, ou, les Essais de la Nature qui apprend à faire l'Homme.' Paris, 1768.
VARIGNY, HENRI DE: 'La Philosophie Biologique aux xviie et xviiie Siècles.' Revue Scientifique, Aug. 29, 1889, pp. 226-234.
'Experimental Evolution.' London, 1892.
DESCARTES, RENÉ: 'Principes de la Philosophie.' Paris, 1637.
DUCASSE: 'Étude Historique et Critique sur le Transformisme.' Paris.
BONNET, C.: 'La Palingénésie Philosophique, ou Idées sur l'État passé et sur l'État futur des Êtres Vivants.' Geneva, 1770. 2 vols.
DURET, CLAUDE: 'Histoire Admirable des Plantes et Herbes esmerveillables et miraculeuses en Nature'.... Paris, 1609.
OKEN, LORENZ: 'Elements of Physiophilosophy' (translation). London, Ray Society, 1847.
MORLEY, JOHN: 'Diderôt and the Encyclopædists.' London.

The French Evolutionists.

M. J. DE LANESSAN: 'Buffon et Darwin.' Revue Scientifique, 1889. 1°, pp. 385-391 ; 2°, pp. 425-432.
EDMOND PERRIER: 'La Philosophie Zoologique avant Darwin.' 2eme ed. Paris, 1886. (Bibl. Scient. Internat., XLVII.)
A. DE QUATREFAGES: 'Darwin et ses Précurseurs Français, Étude sur le Transformisme.' Paris, 1892. (Bibl. Scient. Internat., LXXV.)

LAMARCK, J. B. P. A. DE: 'Recherches sur l'Organization des Corps Vivants.' Paris, 1802.
   'Philosophie Zoologique.' Paris, 1809. Edition, Charles Martin's. Paris, 1873. 2 vols.
   'Histoire Naturelle des Animaux sans Vertèbres.' 2ме ed. Paris, 1835-1845. 11 vols.
ST. HILAIRE, GEOFFROY: 'Principes de Philosophie Zoologique.' Paris, 1830.
ST. HILAIRE, ISIDORE: 'Vie de Geoffroy St. Hilaire.' Paris.

The English and German Evolutionists.

DARWIN, ERASMUS: 'Zoonomia; or, the Laws of Organic Life.' London, 1794. 2 vols.
   'The Botanic Garden,' 1788.
   'The Temple of Nature.' London, 1803. (Posthumous.)
KRAUSE, ERNST, and DARWIN, CHARLES: 'Erasmus Darwin.' London, 1879.
TREVIRANUS, GOTTFRIED REINHOLD: 'Biologie oder Philosophie der lebenden Natur.' Göttingen, 1802. 6 vols.
   'Erscheinungen und Gesetze des Organischen Lebens.' Bremen, 1831. 2 vols.
KALISCHER, S.: 'Goethe und Darwin' in 'Wage,' Nr. 11 and 12. Berlin, 1876.
HAECKEL, ERNST: 'Die Naturanschauung von Darwin, Goethe, und Lamarck.' Jena, 1882.
DARWIN, CHARLES: 'Origin of Species.' 6th ed. London, 1880.
DARWIN, FRANCIS: 'Life and Letters of Charles Darwin.' London, 1888. 3 vols.

INDEX.

Abiogenesis, among the Greeks, 23, 27; Anaximenes, 35; Diogenes, 36; Xenophanes, 36; Empedocles, 37; Democritus, 42; Aristotle, 48; Epicurus, 60; Lucretius, 62; theory of, in relation to Creation, Augustine, 71; Maillet, 112; Oken, 126, 127; E. Darwin, 140; Lamarck, 178; Treviranus, 192; St. Vincent, 205; Chambers, 218. *Between water and land*, Anaximander, 34; Xenophanes, 36. *Direct transition from inorganic* matter, Aristotle, 48. *Marine*, Thales, 33; Anaximander, 34; Maillet, 110. *Terrestrial slime*, or earth and water, Anaximenes, 35; Diogenes, 36; Democritus, 42; Oken, 125. *Terrestrial*, direct from the soil, Lucretius, 62.

Abubacer, Oriental romances upon 'Nature Man,' 77.

Acquired characters, transmission of, Aristotle, 46; Sylvius, 26; rapid acquisition, Maillet, 110; E. Darwin, 145-148; Lamarck, 165-171; Goethe, 186; Darwin, 240.

Adaptation, problem of, in organisms, Empedocles, 39; in single structures, Democritus, 42; in relation to intelligent design, Anaxagoras, 42; causes of, Aristotle, 52-56; Kant, 100; E. Darwin, 150; Goethe, 186; Chambers, 218; Darwin, 234.

Analogy in structure, Aristotle, 24.

Anatomy, Greek, 34; revival of, 86; comparative, Buffon, 132; Kant, 101; philosophical, Herder, 104; Schelling, 104; comparative, Goethe, 184; philosophical, St. Hilaire, 203; relation to embryology, Serres, 213; philosophical, Owen, 218.

Anaxagoras, Adaptation and Design, 42; germs of life, 42.

Anaximander, his natural philosophy, 33.
Anaximenes, his natural philosophy, 35.
Aquinas, exposition of Augustine, 75.
Arabs, the natural philosophy of, 75-77.
Archæsthetism, influence of desires and wants of animals; *upon structure*, Aristotle, 49; E. Darwin, 147; Lamarck, 169; Darwin 236.

Aristotle, relation to his predecessors, 43; works, 45; principal contributions, 45; heredity, 46; errors, 47; progressive development, 48; on 'movement,' 48; teleology, 51; form and matter, 53; on fortuity, 53; on 'design,' 54; on survival of the fittest, 55; on primordial germs, 56; his successors, 58; opposed by theologians, 78.

Augustine, upon science and religion, 19; potential creation, 71; abiogenesis, 72; upon cosmic Evolution, 73, 74; upon organic Evolution, 73; opposed by Suarez.

Avempace, unity of inorganic and organic forces, 77.

Avicenna, Uniformitarianism in geology, 76.

Bacon, Francis, science and religion, 20; failure to appreciate the Greeks, 90; induction, 91; mutability of species, 91; variation, 92; experimental Evolution, 93; artificial selection, 92; gradations between species, 93.

Baer, embryological evidence of the mutability of species, 212.

Biogenesis, Harvey's dictum, 28; Lamarck, 178.

Bonnet, relation to Leibnitz; 'Evolution,' 118; continuity, 119; perfecting tendency, 120; pre-existing germs, 120; scale of ascent, 121.

Branching nature of ascent, Lamarck, 172-176; St. Hilaire, 201-202.
Bruno, sources of his ideas, 78, 79; supposed anticipations, 80; perfecting tendency, 80; interpretation of 'Genesis,' 80; Uniformitarianism, 82; origin of man, 82.
Buch, geographical distribution, 213; direct action environment, 214; segregation, 214.
Buffon, characteristics, 130-131; change of views, 132; conception of teleology, 132; mutability of species, 133; development and degeneration, 133; unity of type, 134; scale of ascent, 135; pangenesis, 135; direct influence of environment, 136; segregation, 136; struggle for existence, 136; imperfect phyletic views, 139; anticipation of Darwinism, 141.

Causation, relation of natural and supernatural, Aristotle, 50, 51; problems of, left by the Greeks, 68; natural, Augustine, 72; natural, philosophers upon, 89; Descartes, 94; Spinoza, 97; Kant, 100; E. Darwin, 148; Lamarck, 163; Owen, 219; 'finality,' Naudin, 224; Darwin, 237-238.
Chambers, 'The Vestiges,' 215; cosmic Evolution, 216; descent of man, 216; saltatory Evolution, 217; perfecting tendency, 217; abiogenesis, 218.
Continuity of Germs (hereditary), Robinet, 122.
Creation, *Potential*, Gregory, 71; Augustine, 71; Erigena, 74; Aquinas, 75; Bruno, 80; Descartes, 95. *Special*, Descartes upon, 94; Suarez, 83; Buffon, 134; Lamarck, 159; succession of creations, Cuvier, 196; Darwin, 232.
Cuvier, early and late views, 195; catastrophism, 196; special creations, 196; discussion with St. Hilaire, 202-204.

Darwin, Charles, relation to the past, 229; changes of opinion, 229; induction, 230, 234; hereditary and educational influences, 231; evolution idea, 233; development of his opinions, 235; natural selection, 236; perfecting principle, 237; 'Design,' 238; 'saltatory Evolution,' 238; survival of the fittest, 239; Lamarck's factor, 240; Buffon's factor, 240, 241; heredity, 242; final opinions, 243; relation to Wallace, 243.
Darwin, Erasmus, principal writings, 139; abiogenesis, 140; origin of man, 141; accidental variation, favourable, 141; struggle for existence, 142; indebtedness to the Greeks, 142; anticipation of Lamarck, 143; primordial germ, 144; evidences of Evolution, 145; transmission of acquired characters, 145; sexual characters, 147; irritability, 147, 148; evolution of man, 149; limitations of his theory, 150; relations to Lamarck, 152-155.
Degeneration, Aristotle, 25; Sylvius and Vesalius, 25; Kant, 101; Buffon, 133, 134; disuse, Owen, 219-220; caused by disuse, Darwin, 240-242.
Democritus, anticipation of materialism, 41; attitude towards adaptation, 42; the universe a mechanism, 42.
Descartes, on special creation and a natural order of development, 95.
Design, intelligent, Anaxagoras, 42; Aristotle, 49, 53, 54; misconception of, Buffon, 132; Darwin, 238.
Development, progressive, Aristotle, 26; Buffon, 133; Owen, 220.
Diderot, relation to Empedocles, psychic attraction and repulsion, 115; survival of fittest combinations, 116; conception of Evolution, 116.
Diogenes, spontaneous origin of life, 36.

Economy of growth, law of, Aristotle, 25, 46; Goethe, 25; St. Hilaire, 25; Treviranus, 190.
Embryology, advance of, 27; evidence of Evolution and unity of type, Meckel, 212; Baer, 212; Serres, 212; Owen, 220.
Empedocles, succession of life, 37; fortuitous origin, 38; survival of the fittest, 39; struggle for existence, 39; relation to modern Evolution, 41; criticised by Aristotle, 55; attraction and repulsion, 37.
Environment, Influences of, Maillet, 112; direct, Buffon, 136, 137; Kant, 101; indirect, E. Darwin, 147; Lamarck, 172; direct, Lamarck, 177-178; Treviranus, 191; action upon early stages of development, St. Hilaire, 199; action upon fixation of type, St. Vincent, 205; Buch, 214; Haldeman, 214;

Spencer, 215; Chambers, 217; Naudin, 224; Darwin, 240.
Epicurus, lack of scientific spirit, 59; mechanical philosophy, 60.
Evolution, *Ceaseless changes* in the Universe, Heraclitus, 37; natural philosophers, 88; Leibnitz, 88, 95; Descartes, 94; Lamarck, 163; Chambers, 216; historic terms, 15; and natural causation, 21; Emboîtement, 26; in terms of *movement*, Aristotle, 50; 'Saltatory,' St. Hilaire, 200. *Still in process*, Empedocles, 38; Aristotle, 48; Diderôt, 116. *Evidences of, in transitions between species*, Bacon, 93; Leibnitz, 96; Kant, 102; E. Darwin, 145. [See also Vestigial Structures.] *Gradual development*, Empedocles, 40; Aristotle, 48; Bruno, 80; Descartes, Leibnitz, 96; Diderôt, 116; Goethe, 187. [See also Scale of Ascent.]
Evolution, Experimental, Bacon, 92, 93.

Fixation of type, St. Vincent, 206; Naudin, 224.
Form and matter, relations of, Aristotle, 49, 53; Bruno, 80; Goethe, 186; Treviranus, 194.
Fortuity *vs.* Design, Democritus, 42; opinions of Aristotle, 53; Diderôt, 117; Darwin, 238.
Fossils, as evidence of past history of the globe, Xenophanes, 36; Leibnitz, 96; Maillet, 112.

Geographical distribution, Buffon, 136; Buch, 214; Darwin, 240; Humboldt, 232; De Candolle, 235.
Germs, pre-existent, doctrine of, Anaxagoras, 42; Maillet, 112; Bonnet, 120; Diderôt, 119-120; Robinet, 122.
Germs or cells, primordial, the original simple forms of life, Aristotle, 56; Buffon, 135; Kant, 101; E. Darwin, 144; Lamarck, 178; primordial spheres, Oken, 126; primordial types, Treviranus, 194.
Goethe, mental characteristics, 181; influence of Buffon and the Greeks, 182; philosophical anatomy, 183; comparative anatomy, 184; unity of type, 184; vestiges, 185; method, 185; adaptation problem, 186; matter and form, 186; theory of transformation, 187.
Greeks, the natural philosophy of, 29; influence of their surroundings, 29; spirit of, 30; phases of their natural philosophy, 31, 32; their legacy to later thought, 64-68; influence upon the Fathers, 69-71; cosmic Evolution, 89; influence upon speculative group, 108.
Gregory of Nyssa, potential creation, 71.

Heraclitus, contribution to the Evolution idea, 37.
Herbert, production of new species by intercrossing, 213.
Herder, influence of Kant, 103; progressive development, 103; unity of type, 103.
Heredity ('pangenesis,' 'perigenesis'), theories of Aristotle, 46; Maupertuis, 114; Buffon, 135; Lamarck, 171; Darwin, 242.
Homology in structure, Vicq d'Azyr, 24.

Inductive method, Aristotle, 16, 47; Bruno, 17, 79; Bacon, 17, 91; and deductive, Schelling, 105; Goethe, 185; Treviranus, 189; induction and deduction, Cuvier and St. Hilaire, 202-204; Darwin, 230-234.
Internal perfecting tendency, Aristotle, 50; Bruno, 80; Leibnitz, 20; Herder, 103; Bonnet, 120; Chambers, 217; Owen, 219; opposed by Darwin, 237.

Kant, indebtedness to Buffon, 98; teleology, 99; Evolution, 99; natural causation, 100; man, 101; survival of the fittest, 101; unity of type, 102; scale of ascent, 102.

Lamarck, relations to E. Darwin, 152-155; life and characteristics, 156-158; change of views, 159-161; conception of nature, 163; of Evolution, 163; uniformity, 165; his factors, 165-167; illustrations, 168-171; irritability, 169; heredity, 171; species, 170-172; phylogeny, 172-176; action of environment, 177, 178; abiogenesis, 178; primordial cells, 178; defects and failure of his system, 179-181.
Lange, opinions upon Democritus' and Empedocles' doctrines and Design, 40.

Leibnitz, continuity and perfectibility, 20; scale of beings, 95; mutability of species, 96; man and the primates, 96.
Lessing, law of development, 103.
Linnæus, characteristics, 128; fixity of species, 129; new hybrids, 130; comparison with Buffon, 130; his method of thought, 202.
Lucretius, relations to Empedocles and Epicurus, 60–62; survival of the fittest, 62; abiogenesis, 63.
Lyell, exposition of Lamarckism, 233; his views, 227.

Man, *Origin of*, Anaximander, 34; Oken, 127. *Slow development of*, Anaximander, 34; in the faculties and arts, Lucretius, 64; in mental evolution, Bruno, 80; relation to apes, Leibnitz, 96; E. Darwin, 147. *Relation to other primates*, tool-bearing hands, Bruno, 82; Leibnitz, 96; Kant, 101; unity of type, Herder, 104; Robinet, 121; Buffon, 134; Buffon and Helvetius, 140–141; tool-bearing hands, E. Darwin, 141; Chambers, 216. *Summit of Evolution*, Aristotle, 49, 51, 52; Robinet, 123; E. Darwin, 141.
Maillet, sudden transformations, 110; suddenly acquired characters, 110; uniformity, 112; marine and terrestrial forms, 112.
Matthew, principle of natural selection, 223.
Matter, see Form.
Maupertuis, psychic properties of matter, 113; heredity, 114; fortuitous variation, 115.
Meckel, embryological evidence of Evolution, 212.
Metamorphosis, *sudden transformation*, Duret, 108; Bonnami, 109; Kircher, 109; Maillet, 110.
Mutability of species, natural philosophers upon, 88; Bacon, 91; Leibnitz, 96; Buffon, 132; Lamarck, 163; St. Vincent, 205; embryological evidence, Baer, 212.

Naudin, unity of type, 223; phylogeny, 224; environment, 224; finality, 224; fixation of type, 224; artificial selection, 225.

Oken, relation to the Greeks, 124; Ur-Schleim, 125; abiogenesis, 126; cellular theory, 126; origin of man, 127.
Origin of species (see Mutability and Evolution) by intercrossing, Bruno, 84; Linnæus, 130; Herbert, 213.
Owen, archetypal idea, 218; continuous creation, 219; degeneration, 219; evidences of Evolution, 220.

Parmenides, 36.
Pascal, influence of the Greeks, 17; upon Evolution, 97.
Pliny, natural history of, 58.
Psychic properties of matter, attraction and repulsion, Empedocles, 37; Maupertuis, 113; Diderôt, 115.

Robinet, scale, 121; man and apes, 121; uniformity, 122; pre-existent germs, 32.

Saltatory Evolution, St. Hilaire, 200–201; Chambers, 217; Darwin, 238; Huxley, 238.
Scale of Ascent, *from the polyps to man*, Aristotle, 48; Bruno, 81; continuity, Leibnitz, 96; Kant, 102; Lessing, 103; Herder, 103; continuity, Bonnet, 121; Robinet, 102; Buffon, 135; Lamarck, 172.
Schelling, deductive character of his philosophy, 105; philosophy of nature, 104; influence upon St. Hilaire, 197.
Segregation, similar in its results to artificial selection, Buffon, 136; Buch, 214; Darwin, 241.
Selection, Artificial, relation to Evolution, Bacon, 92; Buffon, 136; segregation, Buffon, 112; survival of the fittest, Wells, 222; Naudin, 225; Darwin, 235; Natural Selection, see Survival of the Fittest.
Serres, embryological evidence of Evolution, 212, 213.
Spencer, early publications, 215.
St. Vincent, life, 204; abiogenesis, 205; fixity of type, 205; hereditary stability, 206.
St. Hilaire, Geoffroy, characteristics, 197; sources of his opinions and method, 197; his special theories, 198; environment, 199; anticipation of Darwinism, 199; 'saltatory Evolution,' 200; phylogeny and limited view of

Evolution, 201, 202; discussion with Cuvier, 202-204; unity of type, 203.

St. Hilaire, Isidore, theory of limited variability, 207; stability of types, 207; influence of environment, 208.

Struggle for existence, Anaximander, 35; in feeding and propagation, Empedocles, 39; Buffon, 136; Malthus, 136; E. Darwin, 142; Treviranus, 191; De Candolle, W. Herbert, Lyell, 239; Darwin, 239, 244; Wallace, 244.

Suarez, special creation, 83; post-creation species, 84; opposes Augustine, 84; literalism, 85.

Survival of the Fittest, *forms or varieties of life*, Empedocles, 39; supported by Epicurus, 60; by Lucretius, 61; Hume, 97; Buffon, 136; Kant, 101; St. Hilaire, 199; Wells, 222; Matthew, 223; Naudin, 225; Darwin, 236; Wallace, 245. *Single advantageous variations and organs* stated and opposed by Aristotle, 55; Diderôt, by fortuitous combinations of particles, 116; by combinations of organs, 117; survival of opposable thumb, Buffon, 141; E. Darwin, 141; St. Hilaire, 199; Darwin, 239, 244.

Teleology of Aristotle, 51; opposed by Democritus, 42; by Epicurus, 60; by Lucretius, 61; Kant, 99; Buffon, 132; Darwin, 238.

Thales, suggestion of marine origin of life, 33.

Treviranus, his 'biology,' 188; his method, 189; compensation of growth, 190; environment, 191; struggle for existence, 191; factors of Evolution, 192; abiogenesis, 193; primordial polyps, 194; matter and form, 194-195.

Type, unity of, Aristotle, 45; Bruno, 80; Leibnitz, 96; Newton, 97; Kant, 102; Herder, 103; Buffon, 134; E. Darwin, 145; Goethe, 184; St. Hilaire, 198, 203; Archetype, Owen, 219; Naudin, 223.

Uniformitarianism, similarity of past and present changes, Avicenna, 76; Bruno, 82; Maillet, 112; Buffon, 137; Lamarck, 165; Darwin, 232.

Variation and Evolution, Bacon, 88, 92; Leibnitz, 99; *fortuitous*, from sexual union, Maupertuis, 115; St. Hilaire, 199; Brown, 235; Darwin, 244; Wallace, 244.

Variation, fortuitous, *by fortuitous combinations*, Empedocles, 38; Diderôt, 117; St. Hilaire, 199; Wells, 222; Darwin's opinion, 237.

Variability, theory of limited, Is. St. Hilaire, 206-208.

Vestigial structures, meaning of, Aristotle, 45; Buffon, 132; Goethe, 185.

Wallace, on the evidence of Evolution, 226; statement of his theory, 244; distinction of, 245.

Wells, theory of natural selection, 222.

Xenophanes, 36.

Zeller, division of the Greek periods, 32; upon origin of idea of Design, 40, 42.

Printed in the United States
126188LV00007B/160/A